Hank Syndrome Chronicles

Lynn Bailey, MD

Karen Morrell

Illustrated by Stephanie Howell

For information, address to Sisters Unlimited, P.O. Box 69, Weston, Texas 75097.

www.hankstories.com

ISBN - 978-0-578-07106-0

First Edition: October 2010

This book is lovingly dedicated to our dad:

Jim Bailey, *The Original Hank*

and

to our supportive *Hankster Husbands*

TABLE OF CONTENTS

Hank Syndrome Chronicles.................................6

Hank... According to Karen........................ 8

Hank... According to Lynn........................ 11

BIOS.. 13

Hank on the Job.................................... 18

Hank on Vacation................................. 33

Hank "Helps" with the Kids.....................50

Hank and Sports.................................. 63

Hank and Safety................................... 67

Hank Causes a Scene...........................70

Hank: Mr. Resourceful..........................77

Hank and His Hobbies..........................99

Hank and Power Toys... er, Tools 104

Hank "Shops" 111

Hank in Charge...................................122

Hank and the Holidays........................ 140

Hank Behind the Wheel........................151

Hank "on" Wheels............................... 170

Hank and the Kids................................ 174

Hank Eats Out................................... 183

Hank at Home, or Not 197

Hank and His Toys.............................. 206

Hank Remembers, or Not....................... 212

Hank and Electronics...........................218

Hank and Housework........................... 224

Hank and Home Projects....................... 226

Hank and the "Boys"............................240

Hank, Ever Observant.......................... 246

Hank the Criminal............................... 253

Hank in Training............................... 261

How to Submit YOUR Hank Stories..............274

Hank Syndrome

Chronicles

This universal condition of men was discovered and has been studied by sisters Lynn Bailey and Karen Morrell. While the sisters agree certain characteristics prevail in all Hanks, they couldn't decide which version of their individual introductions for the book should be used.

So . . . both are included. To be fair, they drew straws to see whose should go first.

They also debated on the subtitle of the book. Karen thought it should be "I Didn't Think . . ." She cited references such as, "I didn't think you really wanted me to pick up the children." Or, "I didn't think you really needed formula for the baby tonight."

Lynn thought the subtitle should be "The Pleasure Seeking Model." According to her, Hanks frequently are placed in situations requiring them to make a judgment call. Such as, "Should I go to the kids' open house at school or go to the ballgame?" Or, "Should I mow the grass or take a nap?"

After careful consideration, they came to the conclusion that each woman who reads these Chronicles will have her own subtitle, uniquely relating to her own Hank.

HANK...

ACCORDING TO KAREN

The definition, according to Webster's Ninth New Collegiate Dictionary, of *syndrome* is "a group of signs and symptoms that occur together and characterize a particular abnormality."

What symptoms characterize a Hank?

We all know Hanks . . . They interact with us every day. We observe them at work, in social situations, at sporting events, at family gatherings, and, yes, even in our own homes.

Hanks are those clueless, yet well-meaning individuals who entertain us with their antics. They are our husbands, fathers, brothers, sons, uncles, co-workers, and neighbors.

In some capacity **all** men are Hanks.

After my sister got married in 1994, she would frequently call to tell me about some curious event that had occurred at her home. By the time my phone rang, a thousand miles away, my sister had always worked up a full head of steam. She needed to vent . . . She needed to share . . . She needed to preserve her sanity . . . She needed to laugh.

The tales she related had a common theme. Her dialogue would usually begin with, "You won't believe what Simon did!" Since I knew my brother-in-law was a highly competent and well-respected physician, my sister's frustrations seemed all the more humorous to me. In an attempt to diffuse her angst, I would share something absurd that my husband had done. She would then go on to recall in vivid detail something a husband of a co-worker had done, who in each account came across like a village idiot.

And, so it began . . . back and forth conversations between Ohio and Texas. Often our beloved spouses would hear our hysterical laughter. On one fateful day my husband, Bernie, called out from across the room, "Ha, ha, ha! You should make a collection of all the stupid things all those husbands have done and write a book!"

Ha, ha, ha, indeed. His outburst was pure inspiration. As the lightbulb flickered on inside my head, it occurred to me if my sister and I had Hanks in our lives, so did *all* women.

The Hank Syndrome Chronicles became an opportunity for women to share their experiences and to laugh.

Friends came to us with their stories about the men in their lives. Men even recalled their own ridiculous antics, which in itself is another curious characteristic. Soon, we had an impressive collection. We organized the episodes into categories. Our friends encouraged us to publish our collection and to seek contributions from others.

Hank...

According to Lynn

It has been a widely known fact in our family that men suffer the same malady . . . The Hank Syndrome. Men are generally lovable and easy going but have a selective memory deficit and a limited attention span. They are not of lesser intelligence, however, sometimes the "clue-bird just flies right by them."

The Syndrome begins to evolve shortly after puberty when common phrases such as "trust me" or "duh" and "Okay, I'll do that later," start to creep into their vocabularies. At the time of matrimony, the Syndrome becomes full blown and continues to manifest itself in a wide variety of ways.

It has never ceased to amaze me how men can recite the ball scores from every Sunday afternoon football game they have ever seen, however, if asked to pick the children up at a specific time and location, they swear they have absolutely no recollection of any such conversation.

I have determined the Hank Syndrome is not frequently problematic in the work environment. If men work in a predominantly male-oriented business or avocation, most of the males act the same and, therefore, it is not considered atypical behavior. Since women often compensate for men because they live with the same Syndrome in their homes, life at the workplace generally runs smoothly.

We are all surrounded by Hanks everyday. As Karen and I interviewed woman and conducted our research by carefully observing men in a variety of situations, we came to the same conclusion. Much stress and frustration could be avoided in women's lives if they also recognized the Hank Syndrome and learned to laugh at the actions that might have previously angered them.

My hope is to provide women with a fresh perspective. As a physician, I truly believe in the adage "laughter is the best medicine."

BIOS

Lynn Bailey is three years, three months, and three days younger than her "old" sister, Karen Morrell. Don't be fooled! Karen has been known to introduce herself as the younger sister.

Lynn graduated from college at age nineteen, earned her Master's degree at age twenty, served as the space medicine analyst for the U.S. Government, and graduated from medical school at The Ohio State University at age twenty-four. Following a five year surgical residency program in Dayton, Ohio, she began private practice as a general surgeon in nearby Xenia, Ohio.

She has served as Chief of Staff, initiated and still serves as the Trauma Director of the Level III Trauma Program and also holds the position as Chairman of the Department of Surgery at Greene Memorial Hospital. In addition to these activities, she has written classified documents for the U. S. Government, technical articles about surgical topics, and has published medical satire. She also unofficially edited her sister's novels and provided medical details and suggestions to be woven into the plots.

In 1994, Lynn married the love of her life and on that fateful day her family expanded to include her husband, two children, and a lovable dog. For years, she had been amused by the antics described by her family, friends, and co-workers. Now she has the opportunity to experience them first hand.

She enjoys golfing, swimming, traveling, dogs, eating out (a necessity with her busy surgical practice and home activities) and laughing at the humorous things Hanks do. She relishes time with her husband and children. Lynn hopes you'll enjoy her sister and her accounts of "Hank" ever lovable, but rarely understood.

Karen Morrell is the published author of eight books, including four contemporary romance novels, two coded riddle books, a children's Christmas story, and a cookbook. She is a native of Beavercreek, Ohio.

Karen received her degree in Elementary Education from The Ohio State University at age nineteen. She began her teaching career the same year. She founded Spring Creek Academy in Plano, Texas in 1997 and continues to serve as the Director.

In 1973, while still a teenager, Karen married her best friend. They have two adult children, Erin Thomas and Ken Morrell, and six grandchildren. Fortunately, the entire clan lives in communities north of Dallas, Texas.

Karen enjoys spending time with her family, camping, reading, and crocheting. She has made over 100 blankets, donated to Project Linus for children who are in need. Her over-sized purse always contains a novel and a crochet hook.

Early in her marriage, Karen learned it was much better to laugh then to become angry when her husband did something she considered to be completely "boneheaded." She's still laughing.

Stephanie Howell earned a BFA in Advertising Design from Louisiana Tech University and worked several years in her chosen field in both Dallas and Miami. The mother of two sons, she currently lives in Longview, Texas with her husband, Jimmy, and miniature schnauzer, Katie.

Active in her community and church, Stephanie also enjoys reading, writing, and a variety of other creative ventures, including designing and painting murals and, of course, capturing on paper Hank's incomparable actions *du jour*.

Hank on the Job

Last fall, I was involved in a minor rear-end collision. I pulled over to the side of the road but the car that hit me left the scene of the accident. I used my cell phone to call the police and ask them to come, investigate and file a report.

A young officer responded and took down all the information. He told me I'd need to go down to the station to complete additional paperwork. Since I wasn't a local resident, I didn't know the location of the police department. I asked the officer if I could follow him. He agreed, so I went back to my car.

I waited, and waited, and waited. I watched the officer circle around his car, pull out his phone, and make a call. I felt very conspicuous because the lights on the cruiser were flashing and the siren wailed incessantly.

Finally, after about twenty minutes, I got back out of my car and approached the officer. At that point,

I was already late for work. I asked him if he knew how much longer this would take.

He pulled on his collar a little bit and said, "Well, that really depends on how long it takes my sergeant to come and unlock my cruiser." He'd locked himself out of his own emergency vehicle.

And this Hank carries a gun!

For our daughter Stephanie's 18th birthday, my husband and I got her a used car to drive to and from college. The vehicle was in excellent condition with the exception of the tires. One of her first opportunities to drive the car was a short trip to the tire store. I went with her.

The young technician, whose name tag established he was Jason, was more than eager to help us after he determined he'd be servicing the vehicle belonging to my attractive daughter. He smiled broadly as he drove the car into the service bay.

After he had installed the tires, he invited us in to inspect his work. He obviously was proud of his job and was, obviously, flirting with Stephanie.

He instructed us to step away from the vehicle so he could safely pull it into the parking lot. Stephanie and I could barely contain our laughter as we watched Jason open the car door with a flourish and slide into her car.

Unfortunately, he had opened the back door and had inadvertently hopped into the backseat.

Five high level executives, my husband, Harold, among them, recently participated in a lengthy teleconference to discuss an important contract they were negotiating. Since Harold works from home, I kept him supplied with cups of coffee. After three grueling hours, they had meticulously reviewed and made changes to a sixty-four page document.

Upon completion I heard Harold say, "Now let's go over all the changes."

At that time, all five men discovered no one had taken any notes.

With summer swiftly approaching, my husband, Trent, wanted to maximize his vacation opportunities. The only problem was he'd already used his three weeks of vacation time earlier in the spring when we'd purchased a travel trailer.

Always resourceful, Trent bought a new phone, giving him the ability to hold business conference calls by using his laptop computer while sitting in a comfortable chair inside our trailer.

Things went badly right from the start. Having had cell phones in the past, Trent did not think it was necessary for him to become familiar with the applications of his new more complicated device. The first day of our trip was spent with Trent on my phone, trying to get information from a "help desk" in order to use his phone.

Now, he could actually generate and receive calls, with numerous cords stretched throughout the main living area of our small trailer. Trent was all set to conduct business. The first item on his agenda was to coordinate a conference call with six other executives. He sent out a mass email, providing all of them with the contact information.

In the afternoon, Trent was at his post, in his element, surrounded with an assortment of highly technical equipment. Time approached for the all-important phone call. Trent waited and waited. No one phoned at the designated time.

After thirty minutes, Trent was completed flustered. Once again, he used my cell phone, since he assumed his was utterly useless. He got up from his chair, stepped over the cords, and pulled a diet Coke from our small refrigerator. He had no more than popped the top on his Coke can when his phone began to ring.

In acrobatic movements that would have challenged a circus performer, Trent leaped over the trashcan but still managed to dump the contents all over the floor. Breathless, he received his call.

I watched his look of expectation turn sour as he listened to the caller's message. He ran his fingers through his hair and quickly ended the call.

After sitting silently for several minutes, he finally explained to me what had happened. When he'd communicated the information regarding his tele-meeting, he'd inadvertently given the wrong phone number.

There was absolutely nothing wrong with his new phone. He could chalk it all up to "operator error."

My husband, Joseph, frequently works from home. He set up a nice little office space in the sunroom with a beautiful view of the pond, flowers, and birds around the bird-feeder. It's a very serene setting.

One morning last spring, as I sat on the couch in our family room, I could see Joseph through the closed glass door. He sat at his computer desk. I listened for awhile to the others talking back and forth on his conference call as he had the speaker volume turned up high.

Suddenly, he leapt from his chair and told the others on his call to "hold on a minute." I watched in alarm when he grabbed one of the three air guns propped up on a nearby wall. As I now stood with the door as my shield, I saw Joseph jump out the sliding door, take aim and start shooting at the bird-feeder.

My heart was in my throat as he calmly slid the door closed, returned his weapon, and resumed his call. "Sorry about the interruption," he said to the others.

"Was that gunfire I just heard?" a voice asked through the speaker.

"You bet it was," Joseph returned. "Blasted squirrels have been stealing the food from the birds. I've had just about all I can take out of them."

A female voice came on the line. "Did you kill the squirrels?" she asked

Joseph moaned. "Not this time. I think they saw me coming. But I've got another plan. I'll set up a shooting station in my garage." He emitted a low laugh.

"I swear those squirrels see me sitting here working in the sunroom and they take off. Next time I'll shoot through the window in the garage. Those rodents won't out-smart me."

I shook my head as I walked over to my computer. It was time for me to order one of those metal collars to go around the bottom of the bird-feeder that prevent the squirrels from climbing up to it. Hopefully, my purchase would also prevent our neighbors from calling the police.

As youngsters, my sister and I were intrigued when the county highway department came through one summer day and painted white and yellow lines on all the residential streets in our subdivision.

We were even more intrigued when, one week later, the same crew came back and re-asphalted using blacktop to cover those same streets, and the freshly painted lines.

Being the inquisitive children that we were, we asked one of the workmen why they had painted first then blacktopped over it. The man responded that the money was available in July to do the painting and since asphalting is a more costly project, those funds weren't released until a week later in August, so it was necessary for them to do the work in that order.

Even as children, the lack of the workers' judgment baffled us.

My twelve-year-old daughter had an assignment in school to bring in a current event article from our hometown paper and write an editorial based on the information she'd read. She showed me her completed paper entitled, "What Were These People Thinking?"

According to the article, the city had recently spent thousands of dollars on a new beautification project that included four fountains within the rivers that intersect in the middle of downtown.

Of interest to my daughter was the fact that the water, which was being pumped through the fountains, was city water that had been purified enough to be drinking water. These fountains, however, were located and floating in the rivers and the water was being distributed back into the rivers!

"Mom," my daughter had asked me, "Shouldn't someone's mother have told them the way they did this project was wasting money?"

Ah, I thought. If only moms were consulted more often!

A businessman, who lived in Texas, was working with another executive from a company in Maryland. It became necessary to hold a series of telephone conference calls. The Texan was responsible for initiating the call. Not once, but *multiple times*, after several minutes of waiting in Maryland, the other man would phone Texas to check on why the scheduled call had not been made.

Neither man had taken into account they lived in different time zones.

Repeating the same behavior seems to be a common theme for Hanks.

WHAT TIME IS IT?

My nephew, Jim, had just retired after serving in the Army for 20 years. In consideration of how he could supplement his income, he wanted to explore the possibility of turning his hobby of videography into a business. Upon hearing this news, I shared the information with a friend whose granddaughter was planning her wedding.

After meeting with Jim, the family of the bride decided to hire him to video the event. On the day of the wedding, long after everyone had eaten and the reception was about to end, in ran Jim, perspiring profusely.

"What happened to you after the ceremony?" the bride's mother asked him.

"I went to the Preston Museum just like you told me. The doors were locked so I ran all around the place looking for a way to get in," he told her.

"It's the Preston *Auditorium*," replied the women.

"I had no idea!" Jim continued. "I drove over 25 miles to the museum. Then I decided to go back to the church to see if anyone was still there. Luckily, the night custodian told me to come here."

The bride's mother spotted a yellow piece of paper tucked neatly into Jim's shirt pocket. Still folded was the map directing guests from the church to the reception. The route was less than three blocks.

Where was the photographer to capture the mom's expression?

HANK ON VACATION

"Let's go! Let's go! We're burning daylight," my husband called as I was washing the last of our breakfast dishes. I glanced at the clock and noted it was five-thirty in the morning. Daylight was just thinking about making an appearance. Our three school-age children straggled off the couch in the family room, each hauling a heavy backpack.

"Let's go! Let's go!" he repeated, plundering his way to the garage empty handed.

I dried my hands, went into the bedroom to retrieve two suitcases, my purse, and a totebag I'd already loaded with snacks. The kids and I headed toward our minivan.

The engine was idling and my husband was at the wheel. We were in the process of snapping our seatbelts when my husband whipped the van out of the garage.

"Now we'll hit rush hour traffic," he grumbled as he pulled out onto the main street, deserted from lack of Saturday morning commuters.

Knowing I'd filled the gas tank the evening before, I was surprised when my husband pulled into the first service station on our route less than two blocks from our home. "Is something wrong?" I asked.

He shut off the motor. "I'm hungry," he stated. At that instant all three kids leaped from the car. Five minutes later the gang returned. My husband held a super-sized diet Coke and each of the kids had an equally large frozen drink. He got back into the van and then proceeded to offer each of us huge chocolate chip cookies from a bag of snacks he'd purchased.

"This ought to last us until lunch," he said, already munching on his second cookie. I shook my head in wonder. His mother lived less than two hours away. With any luck, we'd be there by *her* breakfast time.

For many years my husband, Bob, and I talked about purchasing an RV. Before we took the plunge and bought one, we decided to rent a small motorhome for a five-day trip from our home in Dallas to San Antonio.

After a short informational "how-to-operate" session at the dealership, we were heading south, confident we could handle the responsibilities of living in our temporary home on wheels.

Our first campground had a lovely setting but an overpowering odor kept us from enjoying the opportunity to cook on the small grill we'd brought. After two days, we packed up and moved to another location in the beautiful Hill Country of Texas. Strangely, the odor seemed to have gone with us.

Bob assured me he'd checked everything and all the hook-ups were secure. He suspected there was something wrong with our rental unit.

On the way back home, after using the RV bathroom while traveling on I-35, our son noticed cars passing us were using their windshield wipers. Only later did we discover that Bob had not closed the valve on the "holding" tank.

This is not a story we tell too often.

The week after school let out for summer vacation, my brother and his wife invited my family to join them at a large rented condo on Myrtle Beach in South Carolina. The only catch was we'd need to leave the following day since we were taking the place of another couple who had to cancel at the last minute.

I quickly organized a family meeting where I instructed our three children ages five, nine, and twelve they'd be responsible for their own packing. I gave them each a list of what to include and suggested the oldest two help their younger sister.

The morning we left Michigan the weather was unseasonably chilly. We were all dressed in long-sleeve shirts and jeans. By the time we reached the beach, the temperature had become blissfully warm. Naturally, the kids all wanted to immediately head for the water. I agreed, thinking that would give me a good opportunity to organize our things. I asked my husband, Mike, to go with the kids.

He was equally eager to spend time in the sun and told me to give him five minutes to change. The kids put on their swimsuits and gathered their beach toys. We all waited in the living room for Mike. We waited and waited some more. Finally, he came out of the bedroom, still wearing his jeans and heavy shirt.

Four pairs of eyes looked at him expectantly. He sheepishly admitted he'd only packed his everyday clothes and had forgotten to bring swimwear or shorts. I quickly put on my swimsuit and took the kids to the beach while Mike went out in search of a Walmart.

As an Eagle Scout, his youthful training to always be prepared had failed him.

My husband, Joel, and I were returning from a family reunion vacation at The Land Between the Lakes. Prior to the trip, Joel was overjoyed when he researched our route and determined we could, indeed, make it the entire way via waterways, thereby enabling us to take our boat.

When we were about one-third of the way home, I noticed a large thunderstorm seemed to be gaining on us. As we were close to running out of fuel, we decided to stop at a marina. Our boat was a rather large cruiser and held 400 gallons of fuel. Topping off the tank was not a quick venture.

There was a nice dockside restaurant nearby, so I suggested we wait out the storm and have lunch. Joel was not enthusiastic and was certain we could "out run the storm." Despite my vigorous protests, we set off again, heading toward our home in Ohio.

Less than a mile from where we'd refueled, our boat took a direct hit of lightning that came in through the radar arch. It destroyed everything electronic and electrical on-board. It also blew a small hole in the side and caused us to feel as if we'd experienced a sonic boom.

Now with only one functioning engine, we could only putter along. Already more than a day and a half later than we'd planned, Joel decided to dock once again. He claimed if he could find the proper parts he could at least fix some of the problems to hasten our trip home.

I suggested since we'd had nothing to eat (without use of the refrigerator or stove) for almost 48 hours he could also stop someplace and bring us back some sandwiches. He reluctantly agreed, but claimed it would only "waste valuable time." After waiting for over an hour, the cab he'd called finally arrived.

Well, instead of going to a restaurant, he decided to go to a grocery store. He returned with a "great deal." He'd bought five pounds of hamburger meat which was almost white from the fat content. He was very pleased with himself when he told me it was only forty-nine cents per pound, thus saving about five dollars from what it would have cost to buy the burgers ready-made from a restaurant.

When I peered into another sack, I discovered he'd spent over $250 on boat parts.

Joel determined I probably had the cleanest hands, although I had not been able to shower for almost two days. He suggested I shape the meat patties while he worked on the engine. He offered to cook them on a gas grill we were still able to use.

Although I did not think it was wise, after the engine sputtered to life, he insisted we immediately get going. I reluctantly took the helm and slowly guided the boat up the river.

A few minutes later the bridge of the boat filled with black smoke. I turned around to see Joel trying to fan the flames flaring from our grill. The burgers and *grill* had caught fire because of the high fat content of the meat.

After witnessing Joel wave his arms and listening to him yell and scream, I could only stare in disbelief as I watched him cover the grill with its lid, lock the lid in place, and toss the entire thing into the Ohio River. There went our lunch along with the new grill Joel had purchased for the trip.

His only remorse was we'd lost a $300 grill. My only remorse was I had not left him on the dock and continued upriver alone.

Last year my husband, Bernie, and I decided to take our two young granddaughters to Disney World for Spring Break. We live in Texas, and this meant two very long days of driving to get there since we were hauling our fifth-wheel trailer.

When we arrived close to midnight, we were told we would receive a discount because the RV area to which we'd been assigned was currently without cable TV service. Since we weren't there to watch television, this was fine with us.

As we pulled into the loop where we'd hook up, an obviously angry man was rapidly disconnecting his hook-ups. Given the lateness of the hour, we surmised cable TV was a priority to him. We waited, wanting to give him plenty of room to maneuver his large motorhome.

He stomped into his vehicle, slammed the door and seconds later gunned the engine. He accelerated and began to pull out, vacating a spot next to ours. We continued to watch as the driver didn't swing out far enough to clear the water pipe extending three feet above the ground at his site. A loud scraping sound was followed with water shooting out like a fountain.

"What an idiot!" Bernie exclaimed. "How could he not have seen that pipe? And these sites are wide enough to park two RVs side-by-side."

Sadly, the damage caused everyone in the area to be without water until late the next day when a repair could be made. Luckily, I'd brought along plenty of bottled water so we could still brush our teeth and take "sink baths."

After enjoying the full Disney experiences for five days, it was time for us to head home. We all settled in the truck and snapped on our seatbelts. As Bernie pulled from our site, once again we heard a loud scraping sound. Glancing out the window, I saw a fountain of water, soaking our truck's windows.

I chose not to comment but our granddaughters had plenty to say when they talked with their parents after they got home! The incident of PaPa hitting the water pipe was the first thing they recalled about their trip to Disney World.

As he packed our SUV with luggage, my husband, Jeremy, assured me he'd loaded everything from its holding spot by the front door. I kissed our children, ages fifteen and sixteen goodbye and exited the house through the garage. I felt assured my parents would arrive from Missouri to our home in Texas within the next four hours to oversee our teenagers for the next ten days while Jeremy and I discovered Alaska.

Our best friends were already waiting in the backseat of our vehicle as eager as we were for the trip to begin.

Upon arriving at the large Dallas/Fort Worth Airport one hour away from our home, I counted the pieces of luggage and soon determined the largest piece containing all of our clothes was missing. Despite Jeremy's protests that he knew nothing had been left behind, I quickly used my cell phone to call home.

Our daughter answered and after a quick glance told me yes, she was looking at our luggage. Although just sixteen, she'd been driving for almost a year and had traveled with me numerous times to pick up relatives from the DFW Airport. She told me she'd deliver the bag. I told her I'd be waiting on the curb and gave her the terminal and gate location.

She arrived just as the last call for the flight was being announced. The airline crew was extremely understanding and cooperative. They told me it wasn't the first time someone had ventured from their home without their luggage.

On a recent all-inclusive trip to Jamaica with our entire family, my husband, Lance, decided it would be fun to try a new form of water adventure.

The four of us, dressed in swimwear, headed for the marina where Lance approached two men standing beneath a large brightly covered umbrella. On a sign, held up by a tall pole stuck in the sand, was a sign advertising "catamaran rentals."

"Do you have one that will seat four?" Lance asked one of the men.

"Si," he replied. "Have you used one of these before?"

Lance shook his head. "How hard can it be?"

The other man stepped forward. "For thirty dollars American money, I'll go out with you. The current gets rough the further out you go."

"I'm sure I can handle it," Lance told the man who led us to a small vessel bobbing in the shallow water.

After securing our life vests, we were ready for our voyage with Lance at the helm. One of the men gave us a hefty shove and we were off.

"Look out, Dad!" our twelve-year-old daughter exclaimed as we headed straight for some rocks, jutting from the water. We hit the rocks with enough force to lurch us all from our seats.

Lance eventually maneuvered the small craft out of the rocks but before too long we were on a sand bar. Our son tried to help free us, only succeeding in losing an oar into the water. Finally, after several attempts we were on our way, too quickly, it seemed to me, heading to the vast unknown waters.

As the man under the umbrella had predicted, the current was indeed strong. Our little boat bounced us up and down, back and forth. Through all the movement, we were heading farther out to sea. Quickly.

Thankfully, in a strange way, we managed to hit some coral in an area of more shallow water. Lance tried in vain to get us loose.

We were stranded for only fifteen minutes or so when we heard the sound of a boat's motor. It came to a stop about thirty feet from us. I recognized the men who'd rented us the boat. One of them jumped into the water and swam over to us. Finally he managed to free us, but not before he'd cut his arm on the sharp coral.

Using his shirt to tie around the wound, the bleeding slowed. He squinted up at us in the glaring sun. "Mr., why don't you swim over to Raul's boat and I'll bring your family safely back to shore."

Lance did as suggested. Raul offered him a hand and hauled Lance into the waiting boat.

Upon returning to the shore, Lance offered to take a look at the man's arm. "I'm a surgeon," he told the man.

"No need," the man replied. "I won't need a doctor. But I could use a plate of food and something to drink."

Clearly appreciative of being rescued, Lance headed toward to our hotel and soon returned with heaping plates of meat, cheese, and fruit. He produced two bottles of water from his pockets.

It was a water adventure our family will not soon forget.

Hank "Helps" with the Kids

AKA "Babysitting" Made Difficult

One July evening, during a heavy rainstorm, I asked my husband, Chuck, to watch our three kids all under the age of six so I could dash out to the store.

When I returned, less than an hour later, I discovered Chuck sound asleep in the family room, a Cubs baseball game blaring from the TV in front of him. The kids were nowhere in sight. From somewhere upstairs, I heard laughter and splashing.

I sprinted up the stairs and into the bathroom. There stood all three kids, soaked to the skin with piles of wet clothes all over the floor.

Upon further inspection, I found out the kids had been very busy while I was gone. They'd completely emptied all knee-level drawers from all four bedrooms and "washed" the clothes in the toilet.

After scolding the kids, sending them to their rooms, wringing out the clothes into the bathtub, and lugging three loads of laundry down to the basement, I ran back into the family room. Chuck was still sleeping.

Needless to say, he's still in the doghouse, or should I say the "outhouse"?

One evening, I explained to my husband, Mark, that I needed to go to work two hours early the following morning. I let him know he'd be responsible for getting our two children, ages three and four, to their child care center. He readily agreed.

The next morning when I left for work, Mark and the kids were still sleeping. Four hours later a neighbor phoned me. She told me both of our children were at her house asking if she knew where their mommy and daddy were. I left work immediately and drove to her house. There were my kids, both still in the pajamas. They told me when they woke up they went downstairs and no one was home so they went over to Mrs. Nelson's who lived five acres away.

Mark later admitted when he got up he went on "auto pilot" and had showered, eaten breakfast, and left for work just like he always does. He'd completely forgotten about his kids.

It was one of those mornings. I'd overslept. As Superintendent of a school district, I needed to keep an eye on the weather in case it became necessary to cancel school. A winter storm had been predicted. I was awake most of the night, in and out of bed, listening to weather reports and trying to determine how much snow was "too much to drive in."

I finally dozed then awoke to see I had less than 45 minutes to prepare for my 30 mile drive into school on snow-dusted roads.

I quickly determined I needed my husband's help with our five and seven year old grandchildren who were staying with us and rode into school with me. Since "PaPa" worked from home and had over an hour to spare, he seemed a logical choice.

I explained all he needed to do was to prepare breakfast of cereal with milk and juice and lay out clothes for the kids. This should have been easy since our school requires uniforms.

Five minutes before our departure time, I dashed into our granddaughter's room to discover a heap of clothes on the floor. She smiled and twirled around, flaring the skirt of the sleeveless dress she had worn as a flower girl last summer.

One blustery Saturday afternoon, I asked my husband, Phil, to take our grandchildren to the public library for a puppet show. "We're all set to go," he announced to me casually as I worked in the kitchen, making ten dozen cookies for our church bake sale.

I turned around. Sure enough there stood Phil and the kids ages eighteen months and three years. Even though it was February in Ohio and a recent snow had left four inches on the ground, the children's coats were unzipped, neither wore hats or mittens, and their feet were completely bare. "Why aren't either of them wearing shoes?" I asked Phil.

He threw up his hands. "How was I to know they didn't get on their own shoes and socks."

One summer evening, before I went out to run multiple errands, my husband, Andy, agreed to be in charge of our daughters who were ages nine and six. When I left, the girls were playing with their Barbies on our front porch and Andy was working in the driveway, trying to fix the lights on our trailer. We were planning to take a camping trip the following weekend.

Andy could not get the lights to work after making several attempts to correct an electrical problem. He told the girls he was running down the street to his friend's house to have him help hook up the lights correctly. The girls said that was okay and they continued to play outside.

They started wondering after quite awhile why he was not back yet. Once it started to get dark and the mosquitoes began biting, our nine-year-old took our six-year-old inside and waited. Darkness fell and still no Dad.

Our older daughter was now getting scared. She tried calling his cell phone but heard it ringing from the bedroom where he'd left it. Next, she tried my cell number. I was home within ten minutes.

Finally around nine forty-five in strolled Andy. He couldn't understand why the girls and I were so upset with him. He had completely forgotten *he* was "watching" our daughters when he got busy chatting with his friend. When I asked him about the trailer lights, he had to admit he'd forgotten about those, too.

TWO weeks after I'd delivered our first child, I felt the urge to go shopping. Although Terry, my usually calm husband of six years, assured me taking care of our infant son was a piece of cake, I was still nervous.

When I returned home with boxes of disposable diapers, powder and baby wipes I was only temporarily relieved to find Terry sitting quietly on the couch with our son wrapped in a towel next to him. Terry looked rather pale and perplexed and didn't utter a word to me. I lifted the baby into my arms and quickly discovered the problem.

Apparently, Terry had attempted his first dirty diaper duty only to discover a stinky mess. The stench overcame him and he threw up all over himself and all over our newborn. Temporarily stunned and now physically ill, Terry grabbed a decorative towel from the kitchen and wrapped up our son, vomit, poop, and all.

Most definitely a case of child care made difficult.

My husband, Myron, is a recently retired Grandpa. One day he was in charge of watching our two 4-year-old grandsons while I went to work. Since he wasn't accustomed to "babysitting", I was reluctant to leave. Myron assured me he wouldn't let the boys out of his sight.

When I returned home, I couldn't believe my eyes. I found the linens from every bed in the house draped over every piece of furniture in our living room. Apparently, someone had stripped each bed completely down to the bottom sheet. Additionally, all cushions from all the chairs and couches were neatly piled together in the center of the living room floor. Curious, I searched for Myron.

I found him sitting at the dining room table working a crossword puzzle. His chair faced the living room. I immediately called for the boys. "We're up here!" one of them called.

"Just let them play. They've been real quiet upstairs all afternoon," Myron told me.

I pointed toward the living room. "Then who made that big mess?" I asked him.

Myron seemed surprised. He scratched his head. "You've got me. I think the boys might have gone up and down the stairs maybe one time each."

I heard giggling on the stairs.

When I prepared to leave for work one winter morning, my husband, Chet, told me he already had his day all planned. Since it was a Saturday, I reminded him he'd be in charge of our nine-year-old daughter. He told me not to worry, he was going to stay at home to work on his genealogy research using our home computer and the internet.

I'd only been at work a short time when our daughter, Kasey, called me to ask permission to play with her best friend. She told me her friend's mom had volunteered to make lunch and supervise both girls making popcorn balls.

The weather was blustery and cold with several inches of snow on the ground and the temperature barely above zero, not uncommon for January in Michigan. I suggested Kasey ask her father to drive her to her friend's house so she could take along the baby quilt we had just finished for her new little brother.

I heard Kasey ask her dad to provide her with transportation; then Chet got on the phone with me. He was less than enthusiastic about having to drive "way over to the other side of town and trying to find Sugarland Drive."

Kasey laughed in the background. Chet asked her what was so funny.

She patiently explained to her dad that her friend lived directly behind our house. Sugarland Drive was one street over from ours. Unbelievably, we'd lived in our house for four years and my husband wasn't familiar with the street names in our neighborhood or the location of our daughter's best friend.

HANK AND SPORTS

Our church has an impressive number of men who enjoy team sports. Many years ago a softball team was formed. Our group challenges other teams participating in an organized multi-sponsored church league.

There was some confusion regarding the first play of the season this year. As a former player on my college team a few years ago, I am aware of the rules of the game.

My husband, Dustin, was the first batter up. He hit a sharp line drive that bounced once and was picked up by the third baseman. As I watched Dustin take off for first, I also noticed our first base coach, Hank Number One, obviously caught up in the excitement of the moment, took off and ran toward second.

The third baseman, Hank Number Two, gave a mighty throw and the ball soared just above the ground toward second base. Not realizing since only one batter had been up to the plate and no one could possible be advancing toward second already, he had thrown to the wrong base.

The umpire, Hank Number Three, called the first base coach "safe" at second.

I sat up in the stands, baffled by the sequence of events. Clearly three Hanks were involved! It promised to be quite an entertaining softball season!

When my husband, Jeff, attended the initial parent meeting that would introduce our 5-year-old daughter to the world of competitive soccer, he was dismayed when no one stepped forward to volunteer to coach the team. He came home that night and announced he'd taken on the job. His first task was to call the parents of all ten girls on his team.

I handed him our school directory with the phone numbers. He'd been provided with a schedule for the games and practice times so he shared that information. This is going to be a piece of cake he'd told me.

After the first practice, Jeff was brimming with confidence. When I asked about team uniforms, he cheerfully told me the group of dads decided to ask the girls which colors they preferred. Although he said pink and black wouldn't have been his first choice, he'd agreed with the girls' selection.

The first game was the following Saturday. I was surprised when I arrived at our scheduled playing field at the number of girls on his team. There must have been twenty little girls all dressed in pink and black. Then I looked at the players on the adjacent fields, all warming up to play their opponents. All of those girls were also dressed in pink and black. Apparently, all the young girls had chosen those colors for their teams.

When the referee tossed the ball onto the field there was a flurry of activity. All ten girls made a mad dash for the ball and through their combined efforts, they swiftly managed to score a goal. In fact, by the end of the game, they had scored twenty-five goals, all going into the same net for the pink and black team.

Oddly, the referee, also a Hank, did not seem to be concerned that he had no idea if the teams were even scoring their own goals or not.

HANK AND SAFETY

My husband, Gary, has an annoying habit of leaving each cabinet, cupboard, and drawer he ever encounters "open" for some unknown reason. Surely he must think they close themselves.

While it's easy to track his trail in our house, it became problematic on a recent golf trip with "the boys." They had rented a condo and per their rules, no females were allowed to accompany them.

During the night, Gary felt the urge to have a snack. Not wanting to wake his friends, he made his way to the kitchen in the dark. He accidentally ran into an open cupboard door causing a small cut on his forehead. He also sported a black eye for over two weeks after the vacation was over.

The women at his workplace were not too sympathetic as they had been closing cabinet doors behind him for years.

My husband, Rudy, decided it would be amusing to play with our son's Epinephrine pen. It was to be used for emergency situations if our little boy came in contact with peanuts as he was highly allergic.

Since Rudy has been a paramedic for over fifteen years, he definitely should have known better. He thought he was playing with the tester that comes with the actual medicated "pen." Joking around with exaggerated movements and sound effects, Rudy took the pen and jammed it against his thigh.

The look on his face when the very real pen's very large needle came shooting out, injecting him with Epinephrine, was priceless.

Needless to say, as a nurse, I was in a panic because of what may happen from injecting a potent medication he didn't actually need. I told him to lie down and checked his vital signs. His heart rate went up a little, but luckily no other problems ensued, other than needing to replace a $50.00 Epi Pen.

As I stood in line waiting for the prescription refill, I thought about the event that had brought me to the pharmacy. I came up with the following: Having a Hank who is a paramedic, $0. Having a Hank who seems intelligent overall, $0. Having a Hank who is an intelligent paramedic who injects himself with an Epi Pen because he is a Hank after all, priceless!

Hank Causes a Scene

My father, George, caused quite a disturbance in church several years ago. He was sitting in the pew with my mother and me. Behind us was the rest of our family consisting of my sister, her husband, their two-year-old son and our ninety-year-old grandfather.

The toddler found it challenging to sit through the sermon and it became necessary for my sister to sit him on the floor with his small car. After losing interest in the toy, he crawled under the pew and tickled my father's leg above his sock.

Although Dad is not afraid of any animals, as he felt the small fingers crawling up his leg, he jumped from his seat and screamed, "Mouse!" at the top of his lungs.

Our grandfather, who was almost completely deaf at the time witnessed the entire thing and began laughing so loudly the service had to be halted until our family regained composure.

Our mother was so embarrassed she would not speak to Dad for the rest of the day.

This event was also featured in the church bulletin the following week.

Why is it that Hanks are soooo loud? It must be some sort of genetic malfunction. My husband, Wayne, talks on the phone like the person on the other end is hard of hearing or something. I tell him, "It's a phone. They can hear you!"

Now my four-year-old son has picked up the habit of raising his voice in every possible situation. Last week in a very crowded Walmart parking lot my son observed a man walking right next to us.

"Look!" he exclaimed suddenly in his loudest voice. Numerous shoppers stopped to stare at the object of his attention. I wanted to quickly retreat to my car when my son continued at mega-volume, "That man is a bad man!"

The man in question shot me a bewildered look as he continued walking to his motorcycle.

The older gentleman had a long beard and long gray hair. For some reason my son must have associated his appearance with someone who is bad. I stopped walking and pulled my son closer to me.

I told him, "Santa has a long beard and drives a sleigh. Is he a bad man?"

"No way!" he declared quickly and loudly. "People with beards are the best!"

His comment was too late though; his words were drowned out with noise of the man's motorcycle.

Living with three Hanks makes for a very loud and often embarrassing existence.

One Sunday last winter our daughter, Vanessa, was invited to listen to her girlfriend sing in a special service at a church in a nearby town. Not familiar with the area, I found directions on an internet map and gave it to my husband, Smitty, who would be driving Vanessa as I was already committed to teach my Sunday school class that morning.

Smitty and Vanessa left a few minutes late, but in his rush out the door, my husband assured me he knew exactly where he was going. I became concerned forty-five minutes later when Vanessa's friend phoned me on my cell phone to ask if my daughter was still planning to meet her in the vestibule prior to the church service. After I explained she should have been there by now, I decided I'd better call Smitty.

He answered on the first ring and told me he'd dropped Vanessa off at the Central Boulevard United Methodist Church five minutes ago. When I told him his destination was the Baptist Church on Stone Bridge Road, I heard the brakes squeal as Smitty did an abrupt

U-turn. He told me not to worry. He'd go back and pick up Vanessa and take her to the right church.

An hour and a half later Smitty stopped by my classroom as my first graders were leaving from their Sunday lessons to tell me all was well. He'd taken Vanessa to the right place, gone home to shower, and was ready to go with me to our worship service. At my skeptical look, he repeated, "All is well."

That wasn't quite the same reaction Vanessa had when I picked her up after eating lunch at her friend's house. She covered her eyes with her hands as she recalled the events of the morning.

After entering the Methodist Church and not seeing her friend, our daughter decided she'd arrived too late to meet the girl. Vanessa entered the sanctuary and sat near the front where she thought her friend could see her. Shortly after the opening hymn had ended, apparently Smitty had come into the church, found Vanessa in the pew, and waved his arms to get her attention. He then proceeded to signal her to get up and join him.

Mortified with embarrassment, Vanessa followed her dad to the back of the sanctuary. Many heads turned to see what was going on. According to Vanessa, her dad loudly announced this wasn't the right church, and she should come with him. Adding to the humiliating experience was the manner in which Smitty was dressed. In his haste to leave the house, and obviously not intending to leave his car, Smitty still wore the plaid, flannel draw-string pants and faded red-turned-pink T-shirt he'd had on at home that morning.

When they'd finally arrived at the correct church, our daughter's friend had just completed her solo and the youth choir was returning to their seats. I assured Vanessa her dad didn't intentionally set out to embarrass her. She nodded solemnly.

Dads sometimes have the very best intentions, but the Hank Syndrome prevails.

Hank: Mr. Resourceful

My husband, Matt, decided one evening when I got called back into work at the hospital he wanted to get into our hot tub. The tub is located on a balcony just outside our bedroom on the second floor of our house.

Matt snuggled into the hot tub all nice and bare. Unfortunately, he didn't discover until the water had cooled off he had not unlocked the door to get back into our bedroom. With only a small hand towel to cover him and a brisk February breeze to add to his discomfort, Matt knew he had to try to get back inside.

He first needed to get off the balcony. He leaped off the deck and landed in some holly bushes. From there he repositioned his towel. Next, he ran around the perimeter of our home, checking all the doors and windows only to find I'd made certain everything was locked up tight before I'd left for work.

Numb with cold and desperate by now, a sudden inspiration came to him. He thought perhaps our doggy door was still open. Unfortunately, because we keep a padlock on our gate, getting to the backyard required Matt to scale our six-foot wooden fence, in the nude.

After accomplishing this feat he found, yes, indeed, the small door covered with a heavy plastic flap was open.

As he attempted to wiggle through the opening he was greeted immediately by our pair of friendly Labrador retrievers. They welcomed him enthusiastically with their wet tongues and pranced on him with their paws and sharp toenails.

Since Matt is a large man, much maneuvering was involved in his entry process. More discomfort came when he was more than halfway through the opening and the dogs pressed their cold noses down his back. . . all the way down his backside.

He was still awake at 4:00 AM when I got back home. He showed me the scratches he'd gotten from landing in the bushes and relayed the tale of his great adventure in re-entering the house.

The next afternoon I had an extra key made for the bedroom door. It's safely hidden near our hot tub.

To our utter despair, two weeks after we moved into our very first house, we discovered the roof leaked. Not having any money to spare, my husband, Sam, and his father decided to re-roof the house themselves. After listening to them pound for several hours and knowing they'd be thirsty, I made them a pitcher of lemonade. I stood next to the house and called for them to come down for a drink. As the duo descended the ladder I noticed they had something in common.

Both men had apparently scooted across the rough surface of the shingles because the seats of their pants were both missing. It was even more amusing to me because we lived on a bus route. The people riding that day had more to look at than they'd bargained for!

My husband, Clayton, loves to go fishing. Although it is not my favorite weekend pastime, occasionally I go with him because I do enjoy the peace and quiet of sitting near the water while I read mystery novels.

On one particular spring morning, the riverbank was exceedingly muddy. Clayton decided instead of parking his truck on the large paved area that was provided for boat trailers and other vehicles, he'd maneuvered us as close as possible to the edge of the water so we didn't have so far to walk.

I suggested the ground looked much too soggy for a such a heavy truck, but Clayton assured me he knew what he was doing. The tires spun several times as he attempted to drive through the thick mud. Finally he turned off the ignition, grabbed his boots from behind his seat, and slipped them on.

I waited inside and watched him slosh around to retrieve his large metal tacklebox and a black plastic bag from the bed of the truck. He motioned for me to roll down the window.

"Here's a pair of boots for you," he told me, handing me the bag. "This mud is bound to cover your ankles."

"Are you sure you want to stay?" I asked, looking all around. "I don't see anyone else fishing today." I pointed toward the sky where dark gray clouds were gathering. "It looks like rain to me."

Clayton rubbed his hands together. "That means the fish will be biting even more. Trust me. It's a perfect day to fish." He closed the truck door behind me after I carefully stepped down. Noticing I could barely lift one mud-covered boot in front of the other, he helped me to the back of the truck and lifted me on to the lowered tailgate. "Why don't you just sit up here and read?" he suggested.

I reluctantly agreed. A few minutes later, big plops of rain splashed all around me. About that same time I watched another truck approaching. The driver stopped on the pavement, got out of the cab and walked down the bank toward me.

"You picked a lousy day to fish," he said, stating the obvious.

I gave a little laugh. "Oh, I'm not the one who decided to do this," I assured him.

The man gestured toward Clayton. "Is that guy over there with you?"

I nodded.

The man suddenly emitted a shrill whistle, quickly getting Clayton's attention. "I just heard on my radio we're under a flash flood advisory. You might want to consider packing it up and calling it a day."

Clayton pulled up his pole, grabbed his gear, and made his way back along the water's edge. "The fish weren't biting anyway," he told us.

The man pointed toward a rear tire of Clayton's truck. "Looks like you're in pretty deep," he said. He and my husband circled the truck a few times and determined, indeed, the level of the mud had risen considerably in the short amount of time we were parked. By now the rain was coming down steadily. The wind had picked up. Fortunately, I had worn a fleece-lined jacket with a hood. Unfortunately, Clayton hadn't thought to bring a jacket.

"I don't suppose you have a wench on your truck?" Clayton inquired as he shook water from his hair.

"Nope, I sure don't," the man confirmed. "But you're probably going to need some help getting your truck out of here."

Clayton sighed and nodded.

The helpful stranger then suggested I wait in his truck while he and Clayton worked on the tire situation.

I willingly escorted myself up the grassy bank and removed my muck-covered boots before getting into the man's rain splattered pick-up.

Several minutes passed as I watched Clayton and the good Samaritan alternate between pushing and steering but only succeeding in getting the wheels more firmly planted deeper beneath the surface. I saw Clayton get out of the truck and pick up his heavy tackle box. Hoping he wasn't intending to resume fishing, I was only momentarily relieved and then confused to see him struggling to wedge the metal box beneath the steering wheel. He gestured for his helper to position himself at the rear bumper.

The next series of events happened incredibly quickly. With the engine still running, Clayton reached across wheel and the put the truck into "drive." The weight of the tackle box pressed down on the accelerator, as my husband later admitted was exactly what he planned to have happened. What Clayton hadn't planned on was the rapid acceleration of his truck.

He had no more than jumped out of the way when the truck's wheels sprayed mud in every direction. Now completely covered in the sticky goop, Clayton and the other man shielded their eyes as we all watched the truck head straight for and right into the lake. Soon it disappeared entirely in the murky water.

Needless to say, Clayton was shocked his plan hadn't worked. I was shocked we'd lost his truck. Eventually we were able to hire a man with a crane who pulled out what was left of the vehicle. Clayton didn't suggest he go fishing for quite awhile. Now whenever he heads for the lake he always parks on the pavement and keeps an eye on the weather.

Being the only female in a house with a husband and three sons, I tend to call on the Hanks in my house to take care of bugs. I found a ginormous spider hanging outside our main entrance and called to my 18-year-old son, Ian, to take care of the problem.

He looked at the situation, walked away, came back with a Red Rider BB gun, and shot it to death. Luckily, nobody got an eye out.

When our daughter was a baby, she was a reluctant eater. She'd spit out most of the foods we introduced to her. Hoping to distract her while I fed her, my husband, Brad, grabbed a toy rattle from the tray of her highchair. This particular toy had a suction cup on the bottom so it could firmly attach to a surface.

Brad impulsively stuck the toy to the middle of his forehead. Our daughter was instantly entertained and I was able to feed her the entire bowl of rice cereal.

The rattle made a loud "pop" when Brad pulled it from his head. Unbeknownst to him, it also made a huge 2-inch round circle that stayed prominently in place for an entire week. He had some real explaining to do to the guys at work!

We had just returned home after a week camping in our fifth-wheel trailer. While I was busy unloading the refrigerator and carrying food into the house, I noticed my husband, Joe, was uncoiling the hoses from an outside storage compartment.

I walked into the house and was immediately greeted by our pair of Labrador retrievers followed by the woman we'd hired to watch our pets. She had both of her dogs with her.

Soon all four dogs were rolling in the grass next to where we'd parked the trailer. It wasn't until our pet-sitter let out a yell, I discovered we had a real problem on our hands.

For some reason, Joe had decided to flush out the holding tanks into the grass next to the barn where we store our RV. Although we were at a "full hook-up" site in the campground, meaning the contents of our tanks went directly into the proper "channels", Joe felt the need to *really* clean out the tanks.

In his effort to freshen those tanks, it proved beyond a shadow of a doubt, there's nothing that attracts four dogs like the smell of sewage.

For our 30th wedding anniversary my husband, Willis, and I decided to purchase a flat screen television to hang on the wall of our bedroom. After bringing it home, we discovered we'd also need to purchase a media cabinet to store all the speakers and DVD player.

We took a good look at the furniture in the room and, after careful planning, chose a place for the TV to be mounted on the wall above the new cabinet. Willis was concerned if we hung it, unsightly wires would be exposed. He decided it would look much better to drop the wires through the wall.

Willis took all kinds of measurements, making marks on several places on the wall. Finally satisfied, he cut a large hole in the plaster. Together we attached a mounting bracket to the wall then positioned the TV.

When Willis stood back to admire his handiwork, he discovered the hole was fully visible, located halfway between the top of the cabinet and the bottom of the TV. He told me not to worry. He'd fix the problem.

We recently celebrated our 33rd anniversary. We have enjoyed using the TV over the years. I chuckle each time I look at the large hole still in our bedroom wall.

Recently, after having minor surgery on my knee, my husband, Marvin, offered to help me with the laundry. As I sat on our bed with my knee elevated and on ice, I watched Marvin bring in a basket of clean clothes. He dumped the contents on the bed and proceeded to sort his week's worth of white socks.

I watched closely as he paired them, then noticed a hole in the toe of one of the pair. He grabbed both socks and tossed them into the trash. Seconds later he did the same thing with another pair. Finally I had to speak up.

"Marvin?" I asked. "Why are you throwing away those socks?"

"You just let me handle this," he told me. "I know what I'm doing."

"How many socks had holes in them?" I persisted.

He sighed and looked at me as if I were a small child. "Two pairs so far," he said slowly.

"How many actual socks?" I countered.

He had to stop and think for a minute. Then he lowered his gaze. "Two," he said finally.

Without another word he went to the trashcan and retrieved the perfectly good "pair" of socks.

I must confess. I love watches. I own six of them and enjoy wearing them interchangeably.

I must also confess I'm a procrastinator.

The batteries in three of my watches had run down and I'd carried them around in my purse for several weeks. As my husband, Trevor, and I were walking into our Walmart after dinner one evening, it occurred to me since I knew Trevor would head immediately to the electronics department to look for new DVDs as soon as we hit the door, he could stop by the jewelry counter on his way to purchase new watch batteries.

An hour later when we got back into the car, Trevor handed me a small blue bag containing all three of my watches. I put the bag into my purse and, truthfully, forgot all about it until the following Monday when I was at work.

Knowing I had a meeting with a client at 3:00, I glanced at my watch. At that moment it occurred to me instead of wearing my large Mickey Mouse timepiece I usually reserved for weekend-wear, I would look more professional with my silver-banded watch.

As I slipped it onto my wrist, I noticed the time was way off. In fact, it was four hours too fast. Deciding the battery must not have been replaced correctly, I pulled another watch from the bag. Strangely, it also showed the time incorrectly. And, so did my third watch.

Curious now, I reset one watch and observed the second hand circling the face. I did the same to the other two. Each appeared to function properly.

When Trevor and I met for dinner that night at a local restaurant I told him about the watches. He agreed it was strange and assured me he'd set the time on all three watches himself, using the clock on the counter at Walmart as his reference.

I didn't think any more about the matter until I shopped at Walmart the following week. I stopped by the jewelry counter and noticed the clock Trevor must have used to set the time. In fact, I noticed several clocks of the same type, all of which reported the time was 10:37. On closer inspection, I discovered the "time" indicator was a piece of plastic, stuck onto the front of the clocks.

All the clocks read 10:37 although I knew the time was actually 6:15.

Obviously, when Trevor had set the time he hadn't noticed it was actually four hours earlier than the "sample" indicated. I pondered this for a moment, wondering how a man could claim to be so resourceful when he hadn't taken into consideration it was unlikely we could have spent five hours in the Walmart instead of one.

Hank and His Hobbies

As an amateur astronomer, my husband, Bernie, decided to construct a telescope "mount" in a cleared portion of our property several yards from the house. After renting equipment to drill down 15 feet into the dirt, he then mixed cement, filled in the hole, and continued to fill the tube-like sleeve that extended above the ground.

A few days later when Bernie was certain the cement was hard enough, he removed the cardboard wrapper and surveyed his masterpiece. His final step was to bolt a large bracket to the top of his concrete pedestal. Our son helped him carry the necessary tools to the worksite.

Bernie soon discovered it took a great deal of strength to penetrate the cement. Standing close to the post, he began swinging the heaviest hammer he could find high above his head. On a mighty upward swing he accidentally hit himself squarely on his forehead. Our son watched Bernie tumble backward, momentarily stunned.

With a nasty gnash in his head and his glasses broken to pieces, I heard Bernie tell our son, "Don't say anything to your mother," as he staggered in the back door.

Our son didn't have to utter a single word. Hank's face said it all.

My husband, Adam, enjoys scuba diving. Although I, too, am a certified diver, we have very different ideas of safety under water.

Adam was thrilled when his brother-in-law announced he also wanted to explore the world under the seas. Now Adam had secured a new diving buddy. Both men were anxious to book their first adventure together. When they suggested a four-day cruise, my sister and I enthusiastically endorsed their plan.

All four of us headed directly to the "dive shop" immediately after boarding the cruise ship three months later. My sister and I decided to supervise our husbands to ensure they were properly equipped and to assure the limits on our charge cards were not exceeded. Our husbands both had reputations of going way over the top when their hobbies were involved.

Their big diving adventure was scheduled for the following morning. I stood by with my camera as the guys waited in line to get off the ship. This was a wonderful photo opportunity as both men are more than a little overweight. In my opinion the "sausage suits" did nothing to enhance their physiques. I momentarily considered the idea of turning the photos into refrigerator magnets, but decided that might be too cruel.

My sister and I enjoyed the large pool on the cruise ship. We had a scrumptious lunch in the dining room then joined another pair of women for an afternoon of playing bridge.

Our husbands returned with barely enough time to shower and prepare for dinner. After we each had placed our food orders, Adam let out a deep sigh. He went on to complain about the amount of "rules" and restrictions the dive master had given them before their descent into the ocean.

"You'd think we were a bunch of rank amateurs," he grumbled.

My brother-in-law agreed. "And the guy didn't seem to have much of a sense of humor either."

"You're right about that," Adam said. "And talk about panic. When you had to make that emergency accent to the surface from around 90 feet down, I thought the guy would have a stroke."

"Wait a minute," my sister interrupted. "Surely that can't be safe, coming up so quickly."

"It's safer than completely running out of air," her husband told her. "I thought my air gauge must have been broken when it kept going lower and lower. I didn't know I'd use up my air so quickly."

I watched my sister's face turn ashen. "You could have been killed," she whispered hoarsely.

Adam laughed off her concern. "That's why everyone has a diving buddy. I was watching him. He shot up like a rocket."

My brother-in-law shook his head. "On the second dive, that leader guy told Adam and me we were required to stay with him the entire time we were beneath the surface."

Apparently, I thought to myself, some dive masters just didn't know how to have fun.

Hank and Power Toys...

er, Tools

My husband, Dennis, came up with an ingenious new way to use his leaf blower last weekend.

He and his father were attempting to clean out the Martin birdhouses in preparation for the spring arrival of our mosquito-eating feathered friends. They'd strategically located the houses near our large pond, anticipating that's where most of the mosquitoes would be located.

We had recently acquired a pair of lovely, but aggressive swans for our pond. When one of them suddenly charged my father-in-law, Dennis grabbed the leaf blower he'd been using and held off the swam.

I wish I'd been home to video the event. I only heard about it from my guys who, by the time I'd returned home from the store, had settled into lawn chairs to watch a baseball game from a portable TV they'd erected on the picnic table.

Ah, Hanks left to their own devises can be quite clever!

When Max first got his power-washer for Christmas, he was anxious to try out the new toy. He looked around the kitchen and I suggested he choose an outside job. His choice was to clean the window screens.

I watched him carefully remove all six screens from our family room windows and line them up against the brick side of our house. He stood back and took careful aim and began spraying,

Sadly, he didn't take into account a "power-washer" was actually powerful. Within seconds, the screens were in tatters. Almost instantly, they'd been reduced to small shreds of screen barely hanging on the bent frames.

Another lesson learned.

Last spring my husband, Max, rented a "trencher" to dig ditches to lay a series of pipes throughout our yard. He'd had a brainstorm to use our gutter run-off water to fill the small pond at the back of our property. He rented the equipment late on a Friday evening and agreed to return it the next day in time for another customer's reservation.

The following day Max lost track of the time. He panicked at 11:15 when he realized he had to clean the mud-caked trencher, load it onto a trailer, and return it all by 11:30. The rental shop was a 30-minute drive away.

Max had hired a college student to help him with his project. Both guys went into overdrive to "wrap things up." In Max's attempt to save time, he quickly sprayed the equipment with his new power-washer.

Satisfied it was clean enough to return, Max started the trencher to load it onto the trailer. Unfortunately, he managed to get the hose from the power-washer caught in the process. With the power-washer in ruins and the trencher hopelessly tangled with the pieces of hose, Max became even more frustrated.

After several minutes of circling the equipment, he and his helper decided to go ahead and get the heavy piece of equipment onto the trailer. I decided I'd better drive him to the rental place since Max was so frustrated he'd been reduced to babbling. He insisted I "step on it" during the entire trip.

Max jumped from our SUV before I could even bring it to a full stop. He ran into the rental office. By that time it was 12:20 and he knew he was incredibly late.

The owner came out to inspect the trencher and told Max he'd have to pay the $35.00 cleaning fee since there was still mud on the unit and pieces of black shredded hose were still entangled in the blade.

The woman shook her head and told Max, "At least you got it back in plenty of time with 45 minutes to spare."

Max looked confused.

"Read your contract," the woman told him. "It says you'd need to have it back here by 1:00."

One breezy autumn day, Brent attached his wooden utility trailer to the back of his SUV to haul a load of trash to the dump. He told me he'd be back in a few hours because he'd also planned to go to the Home Depot to buy trees, as his buddy Dave suggested. John, his college student helper, was with him.

Upon returning home that evening, John came into the kitchen where I was preparing dinner. He looked a little worse for the wear and slumped into a chair. I asked him what was wrong.

"Well," he began, "when we got to the computer store--"

"Wait a minute," I said interrupting him. "Brent went to a computer store?"

John nodded. "He actually went to three of them. He said he needed more memory. Anyway, when we got to the first one, Brent noticed the trailer's tailgate was missing. After he bought a couple of things, he decided to back-tracked our route. We'd driven almost to the dump when we saw cars slamming on their breaks and swerving in an attempt to keep from hitting the tailgate." John sighed. "By the time we got there it was pretty much trashed. Brent then remembered taking it off at the dump and laying it across the back of the trailer."

A few minutes later Brent came into the kitchen and sat down at the table. "You know our little trailer is really starting to show its age."

Already knowing where this conversation was going, I decided to play along. "We just got the trailer last month and it looked great to me," I said.

Brent just hung his head.

Hank "Shops"

On a recent cruise I took with my sister to the Mexican Rivera, we were amused to see a man getting into the elevator after coming back from a shore excursion. We had just been to one of the local beaches. The man's arms and hands were loaded with what looked like large plastic grocery bags.

Finally, curiosity overcame me and I had to ask. "What did you buy?"

He smiled proudly. "After I did some fishing, I went into a Walmart store because I heard cigarettes were cheaper down here. And that's not all that's cheaper," he told us, opening one of the bags. "Just look at all this! My wife's going to be so surprised. She always says I'm not much of a shopper."

"Is that a box of pots and pans?" my sister asked the man.

"You bet it is," he told her. "I also got a great deal on toilet paper, tissues, and paper towels."

It was hard not to laugh. "Where are you from?"
I ventured, wondering where in the world this man
could have lived, obviously somewhere far, far, away
from modern stores.

"Chicago," the man told us.

I nodded in amazement. That clearly explained
everything. Hank strikes again!

While visiting friends 200 miles from our home, my husband, Bill, suddenly decided to go shopping for a tractor. My friend's husband thought that was a terrific idea and suggested they talk with a salesman after dinner.

It was getting dark as we piled into a car and drove about 40 miles to the tractor store. Both men were surprised the store was closed at 8:45 on a Sunday evening.

Ever resourceful, my husband retrieved a large flashlight from the trunk. My friend and I stayed in the car but watched our husbands walk back and forth, gazing longingly at the farm equipment through the fence of razor wire, all the while fierce-looking dogs barked and snarled from the other side of the barrier.

"It's a good thing they're closed," my friend said.

I nodded. "Yes, and I wonder how in the world Bill would get a tractor home."

My friend shook her head. "Neither of them probably thought of that."

"I don't even understand Bill's fascination with tractors all of a sudden," I replied. "We only have a quarter acre in a subdivision."

I had complained for literally months that my 15-year-old sweeper just would not pick up dirt consistently. Sometimes it did and other times it didn't. My husband, Clarence, told me he thought sweepers were made to last a lot longer than that. He took the sweeper into the family room and began removing screws and belts. Dust flew everywhere.

"These new fangled machines," he said. "They have parts that are completely unnecessary." He held up a cone-shaped device. "Just look at this filter thing. Useless. And this," he said as he removed the adjustable height knob. Wiping his hands on his pants, he stood the sweeper upright and proclaimed it fixed. "Go ahead and try it," he urged.

I turned it on and tried it, hoping to pick up the debris from Clarence's handiwork. It made an unusual whirling noise but wouldn't pick up even a small particle.

Clarence snorted. "Those inexpensive sweepers are just pieces of junk." He took his keys from his pant's pocket. "Let's go out and get something reliable."

I truly wasn't surprised when Clarence passed by the appliance store and continued to drive for another 25 miles. Finally, he pulled into the parking lot of his favorite mega electronics and computer store. Immediately upon going inside Clarence grabbed a cart and dashed off to the DVD department. I went off in search of a new sweeper.

After 20 minutes, I had narrowed my selection to three models. Each had a 36-month guarantee and impressive features. They were all priced between $159 and $199. I left the appliance department in search of Clarence. Sure enough I found him with the cart loaded to the brim.

"What's all that?" I asked.

He took off, quickly pushing the cart toward the sweepers. "It's just some stuff for work," he called over his shoulder. Less than two minutes later after doing a careful appraisal of the 20 or so models of sweepers, he grabbed a light-weight upright model and tossed it onto the heap in his cart. "This one looks good," he proclaimed, heading toward the checkout.

I followed him. When the cashier totaled the cartful and Clarence saw he owed a little more than $800, he mumbled, "Darned sweeper."

I made note his superior-quality sweeper was priced at $59.

Later that evening, Clarence had assembled the bargain while he watched one of his new movies in a darkened family room. An hour passed and he called out to me, "Come and get this. It's all put together."

I retrieved it and rolled it into the bedroom to start cleaning. I plugged it in and it roared to life without the aid of an on/off switch. When I depressed the button to lower the handle the entire thing fell to pieces on the rug.

I returned to the family room where Clarence was still watching his movie. I picked up the box the sweeper had come in only to discover a large plastic bag, still sealed, inside. It contained a set of directions and parts for assembly. I couldn't contain my laughter.

"Darned sweeper," I heard Clarence mutter.

My aunt Betty was baking a cake for my grandmother's 74th birthday party. It was an old family recipe for her prized apple cake, made with what she considered to be the best apples in the world.

Unable to drive because of recent foot surgery, Aunt Betty reluctantly sent Uncle Robert to the store with a very specific list of ingredients. She reminded him several times not to deviate from the list. The recipe called specifically for Granny Smith and Golden Delicious apples.

Uncle Robert returned from the store extremely excited. He proudly pulled apples from the grocery bag and said, "Honey, I found these Fuji apples on sale for a much better price than those green ones."

Aunt Betty sighed wearily, realizing Uncle Robert apparently did not know there was a difference. The moral of the story . . . Keep the unqualified out of the kitchen.

My husband, Aaron, loves to shop. It doesn't matter if he's on vacation, at a ballgame, concert, or trolling the aisles of Sam's Club. He's the guy who once bought four pairs of shoes at an airport during a layover because he spotted a great close out sale. He purchased five giant beach towels at the airport in Hawaii as we were flying home.

No item is too large or too small. No location is too inconvenient or remote. Deals are everywhere.

Aaron recently discovered internet shopping. He was beyond excited to tell me he'd found a "special of the week" that had popped up on his screen as he scouted for opportunities to buy. This fantastic sale was for light bulbs which were guaranteed to last for three years of continuous use. The price was less than half of what he normally paid.

He carefully calculated we would require forty bulbs to completely replace all of our outside light fixtures. Not wanting to be short if he discovered additional worthy locations, he ordered a total of fifty.

True to the advertisement, they arrived by special delivery seven business days later. Aaron works from home and was on a conference call in his office when the doorbell rang. He used the speakerphone to instruct the deliveryman to leave the bulbs at the front door.

After his call he went out back to relax by the pool and take a little nap. That's where I found him when I got home from work.

A few minutes earlier when I'd pulled into our driveway, I couldn't help but notice our front porch held numerous boxes, so many in fact, I couldn't see our front door. I stopped the car and stared at three large wooden pallets that held huge cardboard cartons.

I encouraged Aaron to come with me to investigate the mysterious tower of boxes. We soon discovered his latest "great deal" was meant for commercial orders. He'd inadvertently ordered fifty cases, each with one hundred light bulbs. His purchase of 5,000 bulbs stacked over six-feet high. The bill for slightly over $8,000 was stapled to the side of one of the boxes. It indicated the amount had been charged to Aaron's Visa card.

Now Aaron can no longer complain about the shipping charges on a new outfit I infrequently order from a catalog. Several centuries of my purchases could not exceed the cost of shipping and returning Aaron's "great deal."

Hank in Charge

My husband, Oliver, prides himself on providing opportunities for our children.

Our son, Jon, had just received his temporary driver's permit. The following day we left for our annual four-day ski trip over Martin Luther King birthday weekend. This necessitated a six-hour drive (in good weather) from our home in Ohio to the West Virginia mountains skiing resort of Snowshoe.

Midway through our travels we had reached the base of the mountains and stopped to stretch our legs and grab a quick bite to eat.

When we left the restaurant it was dark and the weather had changed considerably. The wind blew fiercely and snow pelted us as we ran to our four-wheel drive SUV.

As I opened the front car door to jump into the passenger seat, Oliver announced it was time for Jon to begin his first supervised driver experience. Oliver gestured for me to take the backseat and motioned for Jon to hop behind the wheel.

In horror, our daughter and I both strongly objected to this decision, but Oliver insisted he could "coach" Jon and we had nothing to worry about.

After spending an enormous amount of time adjusting mirrors and his seat position, Jon shifted into reverse. "No!" Oliver shouted as the car lurched backward. "Just pull forward onto the road."

Obviously, believing his father had checked for oncoming traffic, Jon proceeded onto the road, directly into the path of a small truck, which thankfully was able to swerve and miss hitting us. And so began our adventure up the mountain.

Shortly after entering the freeway, Oliver instructed Jon to just set the car on cruise control so he wouldn't have to worry about varying his speed on the curves we were encountering. From my position behind Oliver, I glanced at the speedometer and saw we were traveling at 70 mph.

Meanwhile, Oliver told Jon to increase the speed of the windshield wipers as snow accumulated on the window. Both of my guys chatted casually about what time they planned on hitting the slopes in the morning and how the new layers of snow would add to their fun. Neither seemed to notice when the SUV fishtailed around a curve on the slippery road.

When my fingernails grabbed the back of Oliver's neck, he began to realize perhaps he had made a slight miscalculation on the severity of the weather and Jon's ability to handle those conditions. Jon didn't utter one word of argument when I told him to pull into the rest stop we were approaching in one mile.

After Jon brought the SUV to a stop, all four of us got out of the vehicle. My daughter and I took positions in the front. Oliver and Jon got in the back. Although neither guy seemed the worse for wear, our daughter breathed heavily and could barely snap on her seatbelt.

"I thought we were going over the edge of that mountain," she whispered. Her voice held an edge of hysteria.

"Me, too," I told her.

"In two years when I get my learner's permit," she began, "promise me, Mom. Don't let Dad try to teach me how to drive."

I heard snoring coming from directly behind me.

My daughter turned around. "They're both asleep," she confirmed. "How can they just close their eyes after an experience like that?"

"I have no idea, Honey," I said. "Don't worry. I won't be able to sleep for a long, long time."

My husband, Mitch, ate lunch at a local burger shop one day last winter. He discovered a game piece on his large soft drink cup. He pulled it off to find the one-and-only ten-thousand dollar grand prize winning ticket.

Mitch took the ticket to the grocery store next door to use a copy machine to duplicate the winning piece. Three hours later our son came home from school. Mitch showed him the copied ticket. Our son asked to see the real thing. Mitch searched his pants pocket. No ticket.

Now in a panic, we all accompanied him back to the store. I watched him run over to the copy machine. Upon lifting the lid, we learned his ticket wasn't there either.

As he and the rest of our family trudged toward the door of the grocery, our five-year-old daughter saw a small pile of trash on the floor and decided to walk through it. Sticking out toward the bottom of the heap was his winning ticket. It was his lucky, lucky day!

My husband, Zack, came in from work one evening and announced, "I won't be home for dinner tomorrow night."

I gave him an incredulous look.

"Don't start on me," he snapped. "A group of us from work are going to get together and I'm going. I looked at my calendar and there's nothing going on."

I shrugged. "Fine," I told him.

"There's nothing you can do or say that will make me change my mind," he insisted.

"Okay then," I said. "I'll enjoy eating with all four of our kids and all ten of our grandkids."

Zack looked confused. "What's going on?"

I continued, "Tomorrow is your birthday and you invited them all over for a cookout."

Several years ago, I traveled to Florida to help an elderly friend move from one condo to another. I had chatted on the phone with my husband, Martin, multiple times daily when in the middle of my third day away he proclaimed, "Your dog is missing."

My dog at that time was a fourteen pound miniature dachshund named Nutmeg. She had the annoying habit of anointing any carpet on contact. For this reason, we had run an electric fence wire beneath the kitchen, breakfast nook, and pantry floors so she only had access to those tiled areas.

Martin remembered he had to feed and water the dog each morning. He also needed to clean up her potty paper as she didn't have access to the great outdoors. By the third day I was gone, it occurred to him her food and water bowls had not been touched since I had left. Her papers were also still clean.

When our teenage son came home from school he'd asked, "Where's Nutmeg?"

Father and son both had to admit they hadn't seen her in days. Martin also told me two nights before he'd heard whining and crying from an area beneath our upstairs bedroom, but he thought it was a wild animal outside. When I was home I hadn't ever heard such noises, so I thought his conclusion was unlikely.

Our teenage daughter had been away at a friend's house for the exact amount of time I'd been gone. Using my cell phone from Florida, I rapidly called all local family members to help with the search for Nutmeg.

Within ten minutes of our daughter joining the rescue party, she heard a faint scratching sound coming from inside the pantry. She opened the door and out ran Nutmeg.

Apparently, Martin and our son had been eating out during my absence, later admitting they'd only gone into the pantry once to pull out some snacks the night I'd left.

Fortunately, Nutmeg didn't suffer any longterm effects, although she'd been without food or water for three days.

Our two teenagers attend a small private school in Wisconsin. My husband, Walt, and I were on the Prom committee. Excited to use his new digital camera, Walt volunteered to take pictures of the event. The night of the Prom he quickly told me I wouldn't need my small 35mm camera when he saw me tuck it inside my purse. He insisted his would create much better pictures.

Three weeks before, on Easter, he hadn't charged the batteries and we missed having pictures of our grandkids participating in the egg hunt at church. I asked Walt if he'd made sure the batteries were strong enough to take lots of pictures. He assured me he'd checked and I shouldn't worry.

Later that evening, when the Prom king and queen were announced, several adults began searching for Walt and his camera. The new royal couple waited...and waited...and waited. Finally someone located Walt. He'd been chatting outside with the father of another student. The crowd parted as he got in position to take a picture. He fumbled for several minutes, then lowered his camera in defeat. His "capture card" was full.

As I rapidly handed him my "cheap" 35mm camera, he reluctantly snapped several pictures then growled under his breath, "Don't even ask," as he made his way to the back of the auditorium. The father who'd chatted with him earlier came up to us.

"Hey, Walt!" the man called. "I want to give you my email address, so you can send me some of those pictures you took of that black Camaro in the parking lot."

Walt hung his head.

Gotcha.

Last week I ran into my friend, Jan, at the Kroger store. I asked her if her husband had contacted mine to make arrangements to go to the newest, latest, and greatest thriller adventure movie they'd been raving about.

Jan shook her head.

"Somehow I didn't think it would work out," I told her. "I happened to overhear Ralph when he was on the speakerphone with John. Their conversation went something like this:

"Say, John, have you seen the latest and greatest thriller adventure movie?"

"Uh, I don't think so, Ralph."

"Wanna see it?"

"Sure."

I sighed and told Jan, "They exchanged goodbyes and hung up. Then Ralph said to me, 'I'll be back later. John and I are going to the movies.' I didn't say anything to Ralph, until I noticed him getting his keys out of his pocket. As he headed toward the back door, I asked him if he'd called John."

"No. Why should I? He said he wanted to go," Ralph told me.

"Humor me and call him," I told him. "Ralph put his keys on the kitchen counter and went to search for a phone book."

Jan started laughing. "Wait a minute," she said. "Ralph and John have been best friends for over 15 years."

"I know. And John's number is posted on our phone as an emergency contact person."

"Oh, my. What happened next?" Jan wanted to know.

"Well, at that point Ralph became angry and confused when he discovered John didn't answer the phone," I continued. "Then I sarcastically told him I bet John was already at the theater. He smiled and said he thought I was right and dashed out the door. I reminded him to remember his wallet and he reminded me he wasn't a two-year-old." I laughed, recalling what had happened next.

"What?" Jan prompted.

"Ralph went out the door and came right back in for his keys and his wallet."

Jan shook her head. "Would you like to meet me for lunch?" she asked.

"Sure," I agreed. "How about Jason's Deli on River Street at 1:00?"

"Perfect," she said. Place, location, and time, I thought. It's all in the planning.

When my sister and I started to consciously begin to collaborate and organize our Hank stories, we decided a productive and fun way to work was to take a sister's cruise. The afternoon of our first day at sea, my husband, Simon, called me no less than four times during the same thirty minutes.

Reception was poor and I could barely determine what Simon was saying. I became alarmed after the third call, thinking there must be an emergency back home. He told me to go to the highest point on the ship during which time he intended to stay on the line.

As I dashed into the hallway, I reminded him in all probability the call would be disconnected if I got into an elevator. He instructed me to take the stairs. Although climbing eight flights of steps wasn't something I'd enjoy doing, I reasoned there was something desperately wrong at home I needed to know.

The signal had become weaker in the stairwell and the line went dead. I had no more than opened the door to the Sky Deck when the phone rang again. When

I answered, Simon raised his voice to full volume. Despite my attempts to tell him it was the reception, not the volume that was the problem, he continued to yell. He told me to hang on while he put the call on speaker phone, thinking this would "help" our connection. It didn't.

It took Simon several attempts during our final conversation which lasted for over ten minutes at international rates, to ask me when our dog was going to be returned home from an out of town dog show. Apparently, he had forgotten our pre-cruise discussion regarding the date and time of our dog, Sampson's, return. Simon didn't remember the phone number for our friends, who had volunteered to take Sampson to the show, was attached to the cruise itinerary and posted on the cork-board next to the phone. I imagine Sampson knew more about the arrangements than Simon did.

As a civic-minded member of our small community, my husband, Bernie, learned of a special election for a new city council position. Having just received word of this last-minute development, he spent over four hours on Saturday morning, phoning everyone he knew in town and encouraged them to attend the 5:00 meeting that afternoon.

Following this flurry of activity, he went about his regular weekend routine which included fixing the mower and eventually mowing the lawn before stretching out on the patio for a nap.

Shortly after 5:00, Bernie ran through the house, shedding lawn clippings everywhere. He was completely unnerved; he'd forgotten about the meeting. Fortunately, he did attend part of the event in time to greet those he'd invited to come.

Unfortunately, he hadn't taken time to shower, shave or change clothes.

Not surprisingly, he won the election as all the other Hanks who attended understood sometimes time just gets away from you. Bernie is still on the city council.

Josh and I had only been married for two months when he came to pick me up from a women's retreat our church had sponsored at our pastor's house. It had rained off and on all day but the weather had cleared enough for us to enjoy a bonfire cookout. The ground was saturated and quite muddy and I was impressed when I saw Josh standing in the family room. He'd thought to remove his shoes before going into the house.

Since my tennis shoes were damp and dirty, I called to him to come outside and suggested we walk around the side of the house to get to our car as it was parked in the driveway. Josh made his way to the door in a flourish and swept me up into his arms. Our group of friends clapped and whistled at his display of chivalry.

It was only when we reached the yard Josh knew he'd made a slight miscalculation. He'd forgotten to put back on his shoes and had walked straight through the mud wearing only his white crew socks. The clapping and whistling got much louder as the others noticed what he'd done.

HANK AND THE HOLIDAYS

It was the afternoon of our annual Easter Egg Hunt. My husband Jerry and I are blessed with ten grandchildren from the ages of 1 to 16. They were all due to arrive by 5:30 and I had to work until 4:00.

When I got home Jerry asked me what he could do to help. I told him I would make the fruit salad, deviled eggs, and potato salad if he would clean our screen room. Since it was such a beautiful spring day, I thought it would be great to eat out there. We hadn't used the room since before Thanksgiving and the dogs had been through the area many times on route to the backyard.

Jerry disappeared into the garage, and soon I heard a "whooshing" sound. It continued and stopped. Then I heard someone start the engine of my car and back it from the garage. Curious, I went to investigate. There was Jerry, leaf blower in his hand, cleaning out the garage. He turned it off when he saw me.

"No one will even be in the garage," I told him. "Why are you working out here?"

He shrugged. "I went to look for a broom and saw these leaves so I thought I'd blow them out of here."

"Why don't you save that chore for after you clean the screen room?" I suggested.

Jerry nodded. I went back to preparing the food. A few minutes later I smelled the distinctive odor of paint. I followed my nose and sure enough, there was Jerry, paintbrush in hand, applying stain to the door that led from the kitchen to the screen room. It was the very door everyone would need to use in less than a half hour.

"What on earth would prompt you to paint this door?" I asked him.

He took several more swipes with the brush then stood back to admire his work. "Have you seen all the scratches the dogs have made over the winter?" he replied.

"Do you have any idea of how many little fingers will be touching this door in a few minutes?" I said.

Jerry nodded, his head hung low. "I'll get to cleaning the screen room," he told me.

I returned to dicing fruit when I heard the sound of the leaf blower again. Looking through the window on the door with the wet paint I watched as Jerry blew two seasons worth of dust, dirt, and dog hair all around the room. At that moment I heard the front door open and the sounds of little feet.

"What's that smell, Mom?" our daughter asked as she handed me a gallon of lemonade.

"Wet paint," I said.

She gave me a leveled gaze. "Dad?" she queried.

I nodded. Then I heard my eight-year-old grandson ask, "Grandma, why is there fur stuck to the kitchen door?"

"Your grandfather was trying to help," I returned.

The boy shook his head. "Something like this always happens, doesn't it?" he asked.

I had to laugh. I could always count on my Hank.

I live with a trio of Hanks. Two of them I actually gave birth to, further polluting the "Hank" pool. My little Hanks are still in training, and their role model tries his best to live up to (or down to, as the case may be) his reputation.

My Easter Sunday with my three Hanks ended with a real mess.

I had spent the day before carefully, and, if I might say so, creatively decorating five dozen eggs. I used paints, glitter, stickers, and an assortment of markers. I got up just as dawn turned the sky into a dazzling display of light and hid the eggs all around our front and back yard.

As in previous years, the boys knew the rules and order of events. Church first, then home to hunt for the eggs. I watched them run around the grass, searching under flowers and beneath the bushes. After all the eggs were found my husband "supervised" the boys while I went inside to prepare our lunch.

After a few minutes, I heard repeated banging noises coming from the garage. Upon inspection, I saw the overhead door was closed, but continued to hear the sound of something pelting the outside of the door.

I circled the house to watch my trio of Hanks throwing the beautiful eggs through the basketball hoop, catching them and then smashing them one-by-one onto the garage door. I quickly learned none other than my Hank husband had come up with this great idea of a game.

What a mess! Blue, yellow, green, and orange egg shells were everywhere. Pieces of hard-boiled eggs had been squished into the driveway by two pairs of little shoes and one pair of men's size thirteen.

Well, the "Hanks times three" got to clean up the mess and I got to wonder, yet again, "Why didn't I marry a Bob?"

As the owner of a private school, I send out a lot of Christmas cards. Three years ago I found some "make-them-yourself" cards at an office supply store. They had a lovely winter scene on half of the front side and were meant to send through a printer to display a personal message on the inside. After I wrote the words and tested the margins to make sure everything was lined-up perfectly, Bernie offered to help me print them.

Less than a half hour later he proudly handed me the stack to fold. Something didn't look quite right. I folded one and discovered instead of appearing on the inside, my message was upside-down on the back cover. A quick look at the stack showed me Bernie hadn't made a test copy. He'd printed all 300 cards the wrong way.

The following year, I didn't want to take any chances. I printed the cards myself. Once again Bernie offered to help. At that point, all I had left to do was put on the return address labels and recipient name labels. Bernie assured me he could handle that task. Glad to have received help, I began decorating our Christmas tree.

A short time later, Bernie had completed his job and offered to take the cards to the post office. I was overjoyed with his offer and continued with making preparations for the holidays and didn't give it another thought. Until three days later . . .

When I opened our mailbox to retrieve our mail, I found 300 red envelopes inside, each with our return address prominently displayed in the center of the envelope.

Bernie had accidentally reversed the positions of our labels and had sent all the cards back to us!

Not wanting to repeat any glitches with our Christmas cards, this year I took on the entire task by myself. I gave Bernie the job of getting our pre-lit artificial tree from the attic and putting it in the stand. Our 9-year-old grandson, RJ, was Bernie's trusty assistant. All went fine until Bernie plugged it in. One entire strand of lights didn't come on. Ever resourceful, Bernie unplugged and replugged the cord. Still nothing.

"Great!" I heard him say. "How long have we had this tree?"

I had to think for a minute. "Oh, probably three or four years," I told him.

"It's bound not to be under warranty anymore," he said.

I wondered if Christmas trees actually had warranties, but decided not to ask.

"Well," Bernie continued, taking the matter into his own hands. He wrestled the tree onto its side. "I guess I'll have to take off this strand and replace it."

Then try as he might, the unlit lights wouldn't come off. "They must have used Gorilla glue on these," he said, all the while tugging at the tree.

"PaPa," RJ started.

"Not now, boy," Bernie replied. "I have to go look for my cutters."

Bernie returned with a tool that looked like it was made for cutting barbed wire. He began hacking away at our tree.

"PaPa," RJ tried again.

By this time Bernie was huffing and puffing. "Give me a minute to get this off," he said.

RJ walked over to where I was standing on the other side of the room. "Granny," he said, holding up a small bag. "I found this attached to a tree branch. I think you use these fuses to replace the ones that don't work."

Bernie stopped his hacking and sat down on the floor with a thud. Piles of broken branches and shreds of cord surrounded him.

"You've whacked off half the tree," RJ observed.

Bernie mopped his brow. "These things just aren't made to last," he told the child. "Why don't you help me drag it outside to the trash, then we'll go down to the tree lot and buy a real tree."

RJ was all for this adventure. "What about lights?" I heard him ask Bernie as they headed toward the back door.

"We'll let Granny take care of the lights this year," Bernie replied.

That was probably an excellent idea I thought.

Russell and I had been married for about six months as our first Christmas approached. Early in our marriage, we pledged to work together as a team. After weeks of shopping for, wrapping, and shipping gifts by myself, I thought Russell could help with the Christmas cards.

I purchased the cards, printed the labels, bought the stamps, then set the project on our kitchen table. After reminding Russell to complete the task for several days, I came home from work and discovered they were no longer there.

Imagine my surprise three months later when I found them in the cabinet underneath the kitchen sink, still in the original unopened box, obviously hidden away behind a large box of dishwasher detergent.

HANK BEHIND THE WHEEL

We live in a home on some acreage as do many families in our neighborhood. On past Halloween nights, we did not have many trick-or-treaters because of the long distance between houses. This year a group of resourceful fathers decided they could assist their kids by hooking up their yard tractors to their small utility trailers. They could haul the kids door-to-door much faster than it would take for them to walk.

When each group pulled into our driveway, I met them with a large bowl of candy and allowed them to select their favorites. Most of the fathers were in charge of 8 – 10 costumed kids. All seemed to go well until the very last group.

As I offered up the treats, I noticed the dad had a Bud Light can neatly concealed by the driver's seat of the yard tractor he drove. He was very happy with the opportunity to plow through the remaining selection of candy, selecting two Reese's PeanutButter Cups.

I turned to walk back in the house as he and his young charges headed back down my driveway. I spun back around when I heard a loud "bang" followed by a crash. Apparently, in trying to open the candy wrapper, the man had somehow forgotten he was pulling a utility trailer. He'd turned too sharply and hit the stone post at the end of our driveway.

Fortunately, no one was injured. He apologized profusely for the damaged he'd done and offered to pay for repairs. Sadly, it cost more than $1000 to rebuild the cement post and stone wall.

My husband, Lamont, was deep cleaning the inside of his car recently on a Friday evening. We were getting ready to travel to our daughter's college graduation ceremony at her campus two hours away. He wanted the car to look especially clean as we were chauffeuring the couple whose son would marry our daughter in four months.

Lamont likes to have the music "rockin" when he works outside. He'd turned up the tunes while he scrubbed, vacuumed, and applied a leather protectant to the inside of his large four-wheel drive. He had the satellite radio turned up so loudly, I could hear it over an acre away while I was at a neighbor's house.

When Lamont had pulled the car out of the garage, he had decided to leave the ignition on as he had preset the radio to his favorite station. As he wiped the under surface of the dashboard and boogied to the music, he didn't notice he had accidentally pushed the gearshift into the drive position. When the car lurched forward, he thought "something was different."

As he peered over the dashboard from his crouched position, he was alarmed his car was rapidly approaching our stone circular planter which was about 25 feet away.

Amazingly, instead of applying the brake with his hand or foot, Lamont thought it would be more effective to pull the car out of gear as it was traveling forward, something I remember him repeatedly lecturing our daughter never, ever to do to a car. He insisted it would "trash the engine."

His technique was effective in halting the impending collision with the planter, but it produced a horrible sound I could hear clearly in our neighbor's garden way over on the far side of their house.

Fortunately, the car was still drivable for the trip to graduation.

Once last spring my dad offered to drive a group of friends and me to our soccer game. As we left the game I noticed Dad was backing directly toward a tree.

"No, Dad! Stop!" I yelled from the backseat. I wasn't fast enough. Wham! He hit the tree so hard the trunk popped open. Luckily all my friends and I had on our seatbelts. Dad wasn't as fortunate. He hit his head on the door, got a nasty cut, and broke his glasses. To make matters worse, he was driving Mom's new car.

During our recent cruise, my sister and I spoke with a woman who was relaxing by the pool.

"I'm so glad this vacation doesn't involve driving anywhere," she told us. "My husband, Harvey, always gets us so lost it's ridiculous."

I nodded and sensed she might have more to say about the topic. She did.

"Just last month we drove from our home in Oklahoma into Arkansas," she said. "We were completely lost for over an hour, trying to find a little restaurant my cousin recommended. I think we'd been on every road in the county and it was beginning to get dark.

Finally, I begged Harvey to pull into a modern-looking gas station to ask for help."

The women closed her eyes and shook her head. "Do you girls know what Harvey said?"

"No," I breathed, hoping she was going to tell me.

She snorted. "He said, 'The moron who works here probably doesn't know where we are either.'" She shook her head again. "Isn't that pathetic? For Harvey's next birthday I'm getting him one of those GPS things that can be installed right into our car."

At that moment the woman gestured toward a man with two drinks in his hands, glancing over the crowd, obviously looking for someone.

"That's Harvey," she told us. "He can't even find me where he left me."

I work in the office of a large tire company. The local sheriff's deputy called early one morning to tell us our service truck had been involved in an accident. I was confused after looking at the dispatch record. We had not received any service calls in the past twelve hours.

I later learned one of service men had used a company truck to try to prevent the theft of his own personal vehicle by repeatedly crashing it to stop the thieves. Too late, he discovered the "thieves" were carrying out orders to repossess his vehicle.

By this time, he had done thousands of dollars of damage to his own car and had also wrecked our service truck. To make matters even worse, when he took the law into his own hands, he hadn't taken time to dress for the occasion. He was wearing only his boxer shorts.

My husband, Scott, is known throughout our family for his unique driving ability. A week after we moved to the country, Scott and I were driving along a farm road, closely following a slow-moving tractor.

The tractor driver extended his left arm from the cab. Thinking he'd given the signal to go around him, Scott accelerated and moved to pass just as the tractor made a left turn into a driveway.

Fortunately, no one was injured. The young man at the helm of the tractor kindly explained to Scott since farm vehicles don't have turn indicators, drivers use standard arm signals. Unfortunately, the sheriff issued Scott a ticket for failure to yield the right-of-way.

Less than a month later, Scott purchased his own small tractor. It had a hydraulic front-loader and a mowing deck behind it. It also had two speeds. A small picture of a turtle indicated if the lever was in that position you would proceed slowly. A rabbit meant fast.

Scott was confident he'd mastered all the controls and had the speed set on the rabbit. I watched him approach our driveway, turn in the seat to check the position of the mowing deck and run directly into our daughter-in-law's car.

She still claims her father-in-law is the only person she knows who has hit a tractor with a car and has hit a car with a tractor.

At Thanksgiving time that same year, Scott's parents came to visit us from Colorado. They had recently purchased a new Lexus to make the trip. Although the distance between our garage and barn is quite long, I always reminded Scott to remember his mom's car was parked in our driveway.

On Sunday morning, we all piled into Scott's extended cab truck to go to church. His mother was talking to his father and I didn't want to interrupt her to remind Scott about her car. Seconds later, we all heard the frightening sound of metal crunching metal. He'd driven directly into the side of her car, even flattening one of the tires.

With Christmas quickly approaching, our son suggested getting his dad gift certificates to the local auto repair shop. I agreed that would be a gift Scott could certainly use!

I was waiting by a bank of elevators at the hospital where I'd gone to visit our daughter and my one-day-old grandson. An elderly woman approached me, driving one of those little red battery-powered scooters. I smiled and held the door for her.

As she slowly maneuvered inside she thanked me then commented, "Don't worry. I won't run over your toes. I'm slow, but I'm cautious." She laughed and shook her head of tight white curls. "Now, my husband, Cyrus, he's another story. He's hit several people and a lot more have jumped out of his way."

I chucked. "It sounds like you both get around pretty well," I replied.

"My, yes," the woman confirmed. "Cyrus and I are both almost ninety years old and our arthritis was getting so bad we couldn't even walk through the Walmart. Our daughter got us a pair of scooters for Christmas. Now we're much more independent."

"That's great," I said as the elevator doors slid open. I held the door for the woman to exit.

"Watch out for Cyrus," she warned me. "He raced ahead of me in the lobby." She laughed again. "Old coot told me to 'Eat his dust' as he zipped past me."

Another Hank, I thought as I walked toward my daughter's room. They come in all sizes and obviously in all ages.

Two months ago I attended a retreat for the pharmaceutical company where I have been employed for over twenty years. An impressive number of physicians and industry leaders also attended.

As a group of us left the hotel one evening to dine at a designated location, I happened to ride in the rented van driven by the CEO of my company.

He was anxious to make an illegal U-turn across four lanes of traffic in order to get to a highly desirable parking space. As soon as everyone was out of the vehicle, he sped off.

I stood on the sidewalk and stared in disbelief as he whipped the van around, not taking time for any of us to close the doors.

An assortment of papers, briefcases, and a laptop spilled out onto the busy roadway.

After the meal, I experienced another adventure. As we exited the restaurant, the chairman of the board emphatically stated he was not riding with our CEO anymore. Unfortunately, his was the laptop that had been smashed beneath the wheels of a truck.

The chairman switched places with a woman who had not ridden with my van driver previously. When our CEO overheard the board chair comment he wanted to make a quick return to our hotel in order to watch a sporting event on TV, this Hank sprang into action again.

Quickly commandeering the position of "lead van" he straddled the only two lanes of traffic, preventing the van behind him from passing. At that point, he was traveling five miles per hour. When his speed intentionally slowed even more the trailing van driver decided to pass. Seizing an opportunity for more fun, our CEO quickly accelerated to a ridiculously fast speed in the middle of a downtown area.

The other driver still next to our vehicle, but now traveling against traffic in the lane to our left, attempted to match our speed, rising to the challenge of our drag race in rented vans.

The chase ended abruptly when our driver realized he'd passed the entrance of our hotel. He slammed on the brakes, shoved the vehicle into reverse, and back up in order to turn into the drive.

The following evening, we all arranged for cabs to take us to dinner.

Last March my husband, Calvin, and I were invited to attend the birthday party for a friend who had turned eighty. Although he lived thirty miles away, Calvin and I had been to his home multiple times throughout the years we've known him.

"Calvin!" I called as we were quickly approaching the subdivision where our friend lived. "Slow down! You're going to need to make a turn!"

Calvin snorted. "I know. I know. Quit treating me like a child. I know exactly where we are." He stood on the breaks and made the turn, then picked up his speed again.

"Remember, you'll need to look for the second orange street sign on the left. That's where you'll need to turn," I told him.

"I know. I know," he said. "I know where I'm going."

We sped past the first orange sign and were quickly approaching the second. After he went by it I said, "You've just driven by his street."

Calvin turned his head to glance in the mirror. "Are you sure?" he asked.

"Yes," I assured him.

He backed up and made the turn. I felt relieved I was no longer needed to provide directions. Seconds later I spotted our friend's unmistakable yellow and white vintage truck parked in his driveway.

I shook my head in dismay when Calvin zipped by the house and eventually came to a stop sign at the end of the street.

"I could have sworn he lived on this street," he told me.

I couldn't resist teasing him. "Maybe he's moved," I said.

"Wouldn't his daughter have mentioned that on the invitation?" Calvin persisted.

Gathering patience, I gave him instructions on how to turn around and look for the yellow and white truck.

Sadly, Calvin has a reputation of getting lost when he leaves our neighborhood. While I know this is a common trait among certain people, it is even more baffling to me when I consider Calvin's occupation. He is pilot for a major airline.

Hank "on" Wheels

On my way home from church last month, I stopped by Walmart to purchase canning supplies. My strawberries were plentiful and I intended to make preserves.

As I exited the store with my cartful of glass jars, I could hardly believe my eyes.

I watched a grown man dressed in a suit and tie race behind his cart, loaded with bags of charcoal and a large cardboard box containing a grill precariously perched on top of the bags. The man jumped onto the front of the cart and attempted to ride it through the crowded parking lot.

He obviously didn't take into account the large dip in the lot that is used to help drain water when it rains. The man's cart bumped down into the dip then he lost control.

Trying to stay safely out of harm's way, I stopped walking then watched in horror as the cart swerved and suddenly change directions. It slammed directly into my cart. Luckily, I had presence of mind to release my grip before the runaway cart knocked mine over, spilling my purchases into the parking lot.

Unfortunately, the "driver" of the other cart did not have presence of mind to leap from his. Charcoal mixed with broken glass and sprawled over the wreckage and the man. His suit jacket torn, and he was obviously injured, but he was conscious.

I quickly pulled out my cell phone and dialed 9-1-1. It didn't take long for the rescue squad to arrive. The man apologized profusely as he was lifted into the ambulance. He insisted I take his name and phone number as he fully intended to reimburse me for my canning jars.

Later, when I phoned to check on him, his wife explained her husband had broken his arm and dislocated his shoulder as a result of the incident. She also told me how he'd ridden bulls when he'd rodeoed back in his high school days and always bragged he'd never broken a bone.

Apparently broncing rodeo bulls are not nearly as dangerous as grocery carts at Walmart.

Harry and I live in a retirement community in Nevada. Our daughter, Maggie, and two grandsons live three hours away in California and usually drive over to visit us once each month. Maggie and I design and assemble quilts to donate to charity and while we sew, Harry entertains the boys.

Because we're able to enjoy their visits so frequently, our grandsons keep an assortment of toys and activities at our house. One of their favorite things to do is ride their skateboards on the flat, even sidewalks in our neighborhood.

One Saturday just after Maggie and I had sorted our quilt pieces on the kitchen table her older son, Bryce, came running into the house.

"Help!" he called in alarm. "Grandpa has fallen in the driveway and he's bleeding all over the place!" That message sent Maggie and me flying from our chairs. We found Harry sprawled on the cement, an overturned skateboard at his side.

"Dad!" Maggie admonished, after we determined his injuries were not serious. "What were you thinking?"

Harry shrugged as we helped him up. "I watched the boys for a few minutes then thought I'd give it a try."

"He didn't stay on for more than two seconds," Bryce supplied.

"It looks like you'll need Mr. Happy, Grandpa," our younger grandson said, referring to the yellow, gel-pack with the happy face we keep in the freezer for emergencies.

Harry looked anything but happy as Maggie and I tended to his cuts, scrapes, and bruises.

HANK AND THE KIDS

Our precious baby daughter was born nearly two months prematurely. Not wanting to miss the first weeks of her life my husband, Roger, and I purchased a video camera to capture pictures of her when we couldn't hold her. When the joyous day arrived and we took Emily home from the hospital, Roger proudly showed our video to his parents. His mother suggested he break off the tabs on the VCR tape so no one could accidentally tape over the events. He willingly complied.

Later in the year, Roger was looking for a blank tape to record a special episode of Star Trek. He grabbed a tape from the cabinet and thinking it was defective, taped over the end piece, therefore splicing the two ends together. He recorded his show. Months later he played the tape for his in-laws and was amazed when a scene labeled Emily's 16th day appeared at the end of the "new" recording. He'd taped over the first two weeks of the only copy he had of his daughter's first moments of life.

When Emily was 18 months old, Roger came home from work and joyfully picked up our daughter. He held her high in the air, and since Roger is over six foot five, that's pretty high. He forgot the ceiling fan was on. Fortunately, she was not seriously injured but did suffer a minor abrasion to her head.

Here's to Hank the Gentle Giant!

Although she's now a senior in college, every time Emily doesn't get an "A", she still blames Dad for sticking her head in the ceiling fan.

I have the wonderful opportunity to teach at the elementary school where my two children are students. I enjoy watching them interact with the other kids. Frequently, both of my sons will ask me if it's okay to bring one of their friends home with us after school.

On one such occasion, my younger son, Jacob, asked if Tim could come to our home for a sleepover on Friday night. Since that was agreeable to me, I phoned Tim's home and spoke with his father. We'd made arrangements for Tim to ride home with my boys and me, then, sometime after dinner, I'd drive to his home to retrieve what he'd need to spend the night. Tim's dad assured me his family had nothing planned for the entire weekend and he'd be happy to pick his son up after breakfast on Saturday.

We left school as planned three days later on *Friday*. I took the boys to Sonic for an ice cream treat on the way home. It was a lovely spring day, so they played in our backyard for over an hour until I called them to come inside for dinner.

After the meal, we all piled back into my minivan and drove the two miles to Tim's house to retrieve his things. When I pulled onto his street I noticed the flashing red and blue lights of a police car up ahead. As we got closer, I saw the cruiser was parked directly in front of Tim's house. His mother stood in the front yard with two uniformed officers. When she saw my van, she immediately ran over, waving her arms above her head.

Not knowing what to expect, I watched in concern as she opened the van's back door and jumped inside. She grabbed Tim from his seat and wept. One police officer was with her and the other came around to my side of the van and indicated I needed to step outside.

A crowd of neighbors gathered around. I was surprised when the policeman began questioning me in an angry tone. Soon everything became clear to me.

Apparently, Tim's dad hadn't shared the information about the sleepover with Tim's mom. When Tim didn't get off the schoolbus, she called school and verified he was no longer in the building. Next, she tried to reach her husband, who was still at work on a lengthy overseas conference call, and didn't pick up his cell call. She also called several of Tim's friends, but since I am a teacher, my home number is unlisted. In a panic, she phoned the police and reported her son as missing.

After an emotional reunion between mother and son, I was only too happy to take Tim back to my house, at his mother's request, so she could have a lengthy discussion with her husband after he got home.

I can only imagine how *that* went.

I had just delivered our fourth child, our first little girl, named Amanda. Three days after we came home from the hospital, I made my first solo trip to the store. Anticipating another baby boy, I hadn't purchased any clothes for our newborn daughter. My husband, Rick, reluctantly agreed to watch the kids while I was gone.

I was in the store less than five minutes when Rick called me on my cell phone. He wanted to know when I'd be home. I explained it would take me about an hour since I had to buy clothes for Amanda.

There was a long pause on the other end of the phone. Finally he asked, "Why on earth would you buy clothes for Amanda?"

"Because she doesn't have anything pretty to wear," I told him.

There was total silence on the phone.

"Rick? Is everything okay?" I asked.

"Yeah, I guess so," he said. "But for the life of me I can't figure out why you'd want to buy clothes for one of our neighbor's kids."

I had to stop and think for a minute. "Do you mean Amanda Smith?" I asked.

"Who else would I mean?" he said.

"Rick," I returned with all the patience I could muster. "The clothes are for *your daughter*. Her name is Amanda."

Once again silence greeted me.

My husband, Marshall, and I took off a few days last month so we could get some much needed work done around our house. I left early the first morning to buy paint and asked Marshall if he would please start getting the two children up, help them with their baths, and put them in fresh clothing.

When I got home a half hour later, I asked him how the process had gone since this was his first opportunity to give the children a bath without assistance. He responded that Daisy had done quite well with her bath and hadn't given him any trouble at all.

"Daisy?" I asked. "You gave the dog a bath?"

"Yeah," he said. "Wasn't that what you asked me to do?"

Just then the kids ran through the kitchen, still dressed in their pajamas.

HANK EATS OUT

My husband, Eddie, has a rather delicate GI tract. He takes antacids at times to settle his heartburn. One evening, he was complaining rather consistently his stomach was bothering him. Strangely, he still wanted to go out to dinner.

We debated for quite awhile on the location for food. Most suggestions from the kids and me were met with, "You know that will upset my stomach."

Finally "we" decided on the local diner which specialized in grilled chicken and fish. After we were seated, the waitress announced the chef had two specials for the day. One was an appetizer of jalapeño poppers with ranch dressing and Voo-Doo shrimp was featured as an entrée.

Despite our protests, Eddie felt compelled to order both specials.

Apparently, heartburn is only considered in picking the location of the restaurant not the menu items. He even claimed he had no idea the shrimp dish would be spicy.

Needless to say his dessert was milk.

My father, Jack, enjoyed getting the family together each Sunday after church for a meal at a restaurant. One particular week, he picked a place with an extensive menu and a small wait for service.

After we were seated, he decided to entertain his grandchildren with a trick that involved twisting a spoon in his hands so it would appear to vanish.

During his first attempt, done while the other adults studied their menus, the spoon slipped from his hands. It became airborne and landed along the brim of Mom's coffee cup. Hot, brown liquid splashed all over the table and all over Mom's new pink suit.

Dad rapidly began reading his menu and tried to look innocent. His act was quickly spoiled when my four-year-old daughter squealed, "Do it again, Grandpa!"

Ah, from the mouths of babes!

People say kids say the darnedest things. Well, so does my husband, Elliott.

While we were taking a weekend getaway trip with our two teenagers to a nearby state, the kids announced they were hungry. Spotting a local buffet restaurant with a lovely park-like setting, I suggested we stop there so we could eat at a table on the patio near a small grove of trees.

After a short debate, it was determined we needed to eat inside because it was "way too hot" to eat outside. The restaurant was packed with the only remaining table right next to the buffet line. The food selection was excellent, and Elliott went back three times to fill his plate.

As he walked back to our table he announced to all who could hear him, "If I ate at this place every week I'd weigh 300 pounds!"

I glanced around the crowded restaurant and it was apparent to me the average weight of the other diners was pretty close to 300 pounds.

Our daughter crawled under the table at that time and our son took off for the restroom. Elliott settled into his chair and couldn't comprehend why fellow diners were staring at him and our family was shunning him.

"What?" he asked me.

I could only shake my head. Sometimes it's difficult to take him into public.

My first date with Chris, the man who ultimately would become my husband, was more than memorable. First we saw a fiercely depicted war epic with scenes that still haunt me today, twelve years later. Next, we stopped at a popular pizza restaurant.

It was late with no light coming in the windows, the darkened interior was illuminated by candles positioned on each table. The waiter handed us our menus and I glanced at mine. For some reason I've yet to comprehend, Chris stuck the corner of his menu into the candle flame.

Whoosh! The parchment paper ignited like a torch. Chris grabbed his water glass and tossed it in the direction of the flames. He missed the candle, but hit me directly in my face. Soon restaurant personnel crowded our table with fire-extinguishers and more glasses of water.

Fortunately, other than the tablecloth, some cloth napkins, and the menu, there was no other damage other than my soaking wet hair. We left without ordering.

Chris claims his action was a result of "nerves." I think it was a result of temporary insanity. It is still fun though to retell the story of our first "hot" date.

Last summer, our grandchildren visited us in Florida for two weeks. Since they live in Pennsylvania, it's always a real treat for all of us when they come. My husband, Ernest, and I enjoy taking them to special places to eat.

On one such occasion, we went to a large upscale Italian restaurant. It was quite crowded and the service was exceedingly slow. In an effort to entertain the children, Ernest came up with a table game. He arranged the creamer containers to fashion a "net" and used folded straw wrappers to create a soccer ball. Back and forth went the small missiles.

Then someone got a little too frisky.

Ernest flipped his "ball" with too much force. It sailed over my head and landed in a plate of Chicken Parmesan belonging to the woman who sat behind me. The sauce splattered onto her blouse and purse. She immediately leaped from her chair and called for the restaurant manager who quickly appeared at her table.

Initially, she'd incorrectly assumed one of our grandchildren had behaved inappropriately. Her anger only escalated when Ernest admitted he had sent the wad of paper flying. With this knowledge the woman's expression soured even more. We soon learned her vocabulary was not limited to just a few insulting words and her voice carried impressively.

Ernest offered to pay for her meal and to have her clothes dry cleaned. She accepted his offer but insisted she and her companion be seated in another section of the restaurant.

During our forty-six years of marriage I've had the opportunity to witness my husband handle delicate situations. Most involve other people however. Ernest is a retired District Judge.

I'd been concerned about my husband, Gordon, for about a month. Although his appetite seemed to be decreasing, his waistline seemed to be increasing. One Saturday afternoon my concerns were put to rest when I became aware of Gordon's new routine.

We had just left the grocery store, with Gordon behind the wheel, when he suddenly asked, "What time is it?"

I glanced at the clock, clearly visible next to the steering wheel. "Three- fifty-three," I told him.

"Hold on," he told me, swerving through traffic, rounding a corner and whipping the car into a new Sonic Drive-in restaurant. He screeched to a halt, barely missing the speaker stand and immediately lowered the window and pressed the red button. "You want anything?" he asked, nearly breathless.

"I don't know," I replied. "What's good here?"

"What's good?" he returned. "Everything. I've sampled nearly the whole menu."

"I'll have an unsweetened iced tea," I told him.

"Good," he said. "There's two minutes left in the happy hour. Drinks are half price until four o'clock."

I listened as he ordered. "I'll have a large unsweetened tea, large chili-cheese fries, large onion rings, and a large Diet Coke."

"Do you eat here often?" I asked after the voice in the speaker announced his total.

"As often as I can. It's a heck of a deal, getting my drink at half price."

I no longer worry about the lack of Gordon's appetite at dinner time. I'm also glad he makes weight-conscious choices when selecting his beverages.

My husband, Douglas, is a prominent attorney. He's also quite resourceful. One Sunday evening when our two teenage sons asked the proverbial question, "What's for dinner?" my husband took the chore into his own hands. "Where's the phone book?" he asked.

"Which one?" I replied, knowing in the Dallas Metroplex area we had 7 large phone books.

By that time, Douglas had already discovered the towering stack of phone directories on the shelf above the phone in the kitchen. I watched in amusement as he looked through first one and then another, scattering them all over the counter as he discarded one. "Why do we have all of these? I can't find a thing in any of them."

"What are you looking for?" I questioned.

He turned to face me, obviously frustrated. "I'm looking for the number for that pizza place down the street."

Without saying a word, I pointed to the 6-inch magnet shaped like a slice of pizza that had hung on our refrigerator door since we moved into the house five years ago.

I watched Douglas grab the magnet and stuff it into his pants pocket as he walked toward the garage. I heard the door open, close, then open again. I didn't say a word but had to snicker when he came back in for his wallet and keys.

As I placed the phone books back onto the shelf, I wondered how he planned to order our dinner. He still hadn't made the call nor had he asked the boys or me what kind of pizzas we'd like. Oh well, I reasoned, the people at the pizza place would be able to help him. He was probably there by now.

My husband, Brian, likes his Sunday morning routine. He rises early to read the newspaper while I get up and call a local diner to order each of us the 2-egg breakfast special. My husband drives over to pick it up.

One particular Sunday, Brian was supposed to meet a friend early before church and I was still asleep. He told me he'd take care of breakfast. He certainly did.

After a brief meeting with the buddy, Brian jumped into his truck and drove to the diner. He became upset when they didn't have his order ready. After speaking with the manager, it was determined he hadn't phoned in the order.

I guess his instinct to feed was stronger than his ability to perform telepathy.

HANK AT HOME, OR NOT

One evening during dinner, my husband, Donald, announced he thought I was using too much hot water when I did the laundry. He believed this was causing his pants to shrink.

Immediately after we finished our meal he insisted I follow him up to the bedroom where he'd laid four pair of khaki pants out on the bed. Our two children ages six and seven watched with alarm as they didn't want their clothes to become smaller.

"Just look at these pants," he said, holding up one pair. He quickly discarded them and selected another pair. "These look even smaller. I don't know what you've done to them, but unless you get that problem solved, we're all going to be out of clothes."

"Maybe Grandma should start washing our clothes," our daughter suggested.

Not recalling recently laundering so many pair of Donald's khaki pants, I moved in for a closer inspection. My "big" problem became readily apparent.

"Donald," I said, holding up the smallest pants for him to get a better view. "Take a look at this tag. What size do you see?"

Donald narrowed his gaze. "Those look like a 32," he confirmed.

"What about the other ones?" I asked, holding up one pair after another.

Donald took a quick look then stomped off, obviously no longer interested in carrying on about my skills as a laundress.

Our daughter, however, was intrigued. "These are all different sizes, Mommy," she said. "It's like skip counting by twos . . . 32, 34, 36, 38. What size does Daddy really wear?"

"He's up to a 40 now," I told her.

"Wow!" she exclaimed. "How high up do they go?"

"You'll have to ask your father," I suggested.

After a particularly hectic work week, I was delighted when my husband, Fred, offered to make me breakfast and serve it to me in bed. He asked me what I wanted. I told him a slice of toast with orange marmalade would be great.

As I lingered beneath the covers for a few more minutes, I heard Fred open the back door to let the dogs out. Then I heard him open the front door, obviously to get the newspaper.

He returned to the house a short time later. I continued to listen and heard cupboard doors opening and closing. And I waited...and waited...and waited.

After about 20 minutes the smell of pipe tobacco drifted into the bedroom. Curious, I put on my robe.

I found Fred in the screen room just off the kitchen. He was engrossed in an article in the paper and didn't hear me approach. I watched him alternate between smoking his pipe, sipping his coffee, and munching on his toast.

So much for my breakfast in bed.

When we moved to the country four years ago, the property on which we built our home had only a few trees. In the fall my husband, Dave, purchased 45 trees from a local nursery. Two weeks later he bought another 25 trees from Home Depot.

Not having enough time to actually plant the trees, he hired and supervised a pair of high school boys hefting shovels and pushing wheelbarrows. After two long weekend days of watching the young men plant, Dave marveled that in just a few years we would have a nicely shaded yard.

He and I examined our budget and determined he had significantly overspent on all those trees. We agreed not to buy any more until the following year.

A week later, we received a birthday party invitation for a member of our church group who was turning 40. Having spent a great deal of time at the Home Depot, Dave suggested we buy our friend a gift card from the large store. I agreed that was an excellent idea.

A week later on Saturday, I asked Dave if he would go to the Home Depot to buy the gift. He was happy to do so. He commented he hoped someone would be thoughtful enough to get him one of those gift cards someday.

Two hours later Dave returned home. The back of his truck was filled with fruit trees of several varieties. He proudly told me someday we'd have our own orchard.

I stared at him in amazement then asked him for the gift card so I could include it with the note I'd written to our friend.

Reluctantly Dave told me he'd forgotten to buy the gift card.

As a point of reference, I don't think Hanks should go to Home Depot alone.

When we moved into our new home many years ago, my husband, Curtis, insisted he "needed" the larger of our two master bedroom closets. He reasoned since he was larger than I am his clothes were also larger and he required more space.

Not wanting to rock the boat so early in our new marriage, I hesitantly agreed.

Over time I avoided entering his closet for fear of coming into contact with something which would surely cause an argument. Curtis has a habit of *never* wanting to throw anything away.

One day I overheard our son asking Curtis if he could borrow one of his ties for an upcoming school dance. Curtis readily agreed and told our son to go on up and pick one out himself. Our nine-year-old daughter accompanied him, hoping to participate in outfitting her brother for this major social event.

Soon I heard squeals of laughter coming from upstairs. When I investigated I found our daughter had gone "exploring." She was more than happy to model her new outfit. The ensemble included a pair of red gym shorts sporting the name of Curtis' junior high basketball team, a faded tee shirt with hand-written letters "Spring Break 1972", bright green and purple Mardi Gras beads, and a ratty-looking straw hat that had more than lost its shape. I told her not to move as I quickly fetched my camera.

The following weekend Curtis delivered ten 30-gallon white trash bags of "treasures" to our church for their annual yard sale.

My son, Benjamin, gave me quite a scare when I flew down to visit him and his family a few months ago. I live in Pennsylvania and Benjamin was transferred to Houston several years ago. Whenever I visit, he always asks me to make some of his favorite comfort food meals which I made him as a child.

On one such day, I'd spent all morning preparing home-made dumplings. Benjamin assured me he'd be home early, by 4:00 at the latest he'd said. When he hadn't come home by 5:30, I asked his wife Marie to call his office to see if he'd been delayed. A co-worker answered Benjamin's phone and told us he'd left the office around 3:00.

We tried to reach him on his cell phone only to discover it in the dry cleaning bin, ringing away in the pocket of his pants he'd worn the day before.

When he hadn't arrive home by 6:30, Marie gathered the children to the table and we all ate less than appetizing chicken and dumplings. Finally at 7:30 in walked my son. He could probably tell from my expression I was none too pleased. He immediately launched into his story, trying to justify his tardiness.

It seems he did leave work early. Then, instead of coming right home, he went to one of those mega electronics stores to get some part for his computer. Well, they were out of that particular part, so Benjamin went to another location of the same store. This place was located on the other side of town. By the time he'd finished his transaction, he'd found himself in bumper-to-bumper rush-hour traffic in Houston.

He was very apologetic he'd missed eating with us. I wasn't too apologetic when I warmed some canned soup for his dinner.

HANK AND HIS TOYS

My husband, Clark, had always wanted a boat, but it was not in our budget. He was absolutely thrilled when his father, who lived 750 miles away, offered to give Clark his boat. Well, in light of this traveling emergency, the following week Clark took off work so we could retrieve the boat.

I was only a bit surprised when I saw the boat. At least 25 years old, it had no seats, a non-working motor, and at least one rotten sideboard. The wooden trailer it was perched on had two flat tires. Curiously, it did have a very expensive-looking canvas cover that actually snapped into place, thereby protecting it from the elements.

Clark assured me the boat was travel-worthy and we'd have no difficulty towing it home once the trailer tires were inflated.

All was fine for the first hour into our trip. It was necessary for us to pull into the first rest stop we encountered because Clark had consumed numerous cups of coffee before leaving. He stated he did not want to feel drowsy on the drive he fully intended to make all in one day.

After using the facilities, Clark felt like he needed a little rest, so he asked me to drive. That was when the trouble started. As I was accelerating down the ramp to enter the interstate, I checked my rearview mirror to see the boat on its trailer passing me on the left.

I slammed on the brakes and yelled to wake Clark, who'd already gone to sleep. He was shocked to see the boat overturned in a ditch. I pulled over so he could assess the damage.

We soon discovered the hitch Clark had used was so rusty the pin holding it together hadn't held. He also failed to attach the safety chains between the trailer and our truck. So, off went the trailer.

It's been ten years since our experience with "boating" and Clark hasn't mentioned getting a boat since.

Several years ago, right out of the blue, my husband, Stuart, decided he needed a rifle. He told me he'd been on a shooting team in elementary school and he really enjoyed it then. I gently reminded him at age fifty-four, it had been quite a few years since he was a schoolboy.

No amount of reasoning could dissuade him. Stuart "needed" a rifle. He searched on the internet for the "best one" relying on advertisements from gun manufactures for advise. Finally, he narrowed his selection to a 7 mm model with an expensive scope and a claim that, "You can kill anything smaller than an elephant at 800 yards."

I thought about this for awhile. I couldn't imagine the large game hunting opportunities would be great near our home in suburban Columbus, Ohio. I shared my concern for his potential lack of "wild game"in our neighborhood.

"You just don't understand," he'd told me. "I've always wanted a gun."

This proclamation came from a guy who used a have-a-heart trap to catch mice in our attic. He once slammed on his brakes so hard while zipping down his mother's driveway, he threw her from the seat, knocking her to the floor, all to avoid hitting a toad. He swerves to miss hitting worms after a rainstorm.

Yet, despite all of this, Stuart was determined to buy a gun.

On the red-letter day the new toy, er gun, arrived, Stuart pulled it from the large black box with reverence. He laid down bath towels before placing the weapon in the middle of our kitchen table. He was then off to the sporting goods store. With enthusiasm, he purchased four boxes of ammunition. The "ammo" looked like small missiles. I didn't think they looked like something civilians could purchase.

The next day he convinced a friend from work to accompany him to a shooting range eighty miles away, claiming he needed to "sight in the scope."

Stuart returned four hours later. I didn't comment when I saw him rubbing his right shoulder. Somehow I also held my words that evening as he tried to conceal a heating pad beneath his sweatshirt while he watched TV.

Two weeks passed and the rifle still occupied its position on the kitchen table. With Easter approaching, I placed the gun back into its case and put it in the back of Stuart's closet.

It's been over five years since his "big game" experience. I wonder if bullets have a shelf-life like cans of soup?

HANK REMEMBERS, OR NOT

My husband, Oscar, came to a startling revelation last week. He had recently purchased a brand new car and was upset when a spring rainstorm left it spotted.

As he drove into our local car wash, he realized the attendant had not folded in his side view mirrors. Recalling he had an inside control to maneuver the mirrors, he quickly hit the master button.

It wasn't until the automatic traction pulled his car into the wash he realized he'd accidentally hit the wrong button. He discovered too late he'd lowered all the windows. The thick soap began spraying him and thoroughly soaking the interior of his car.

Oscar was also dismayed to find out the soap was not only pungent but also extremely sticky. It was necessary for him to return home, shower, completely change his clothes, send his suit to the cleaners, and have the inside of his car detailed.

The total cost of the inaugural wash for his new car was $175.

I had recently completed my Master's degree in nursing and decided to take the plunge and apply for a PhD program. The school I hoped to attend encouraged married candidates to include their spouses when they came for the initial in-depth interview as well as to evaluate the couple to determine their commitment to the program.

I gave my husband, Rick, over a month notice. I needed him to take off work and travel with me from our home in Ohio to Tennessee for the interview. I carefully marked the dates on the calendar hanging next to the phone in our kitchen as well as the calendar on the desk in his home office. I also reminded him several times to which he always replied, "I've got it! I've got it! I know when I'm supposed to go with you."

Since Rick owns his own spa installation company, he decided to close the business for that particular Monday. We'd planned to leave on a Sunday, interview on Monday and drive home that night.

Two weeks before, I heard Rick on the phone one evening, speaking rapidly, obviously making arrangements with first one employee and then another, notifying them that they were all off on the "appropriate" Monday.

I thought it was odd he began scurrying around the house, getting things organized two weeks before our upcoming trip.

When my curiosity overcame me, I asked Rick why he was rushing around two weeks before we were supposed to leave. He stopped in his tracks and stared me at. "No," he said with conviction. "It is *this* weekend."

I reminded him of the dates, both the current date and the one I'd circled on the calendars. He replied, "They must have changed the date because I have already given everybody off at work this upcoming Monday and that is when I'm available to go to Tennessee with you."

My interview was indeed scheduled for ten days later. Rick halted his packing effort. "Well, then I'm just not going to be able to go because I've already given the guys off and now I can't tell them they have to work. I've got a schedule to keep."

I attended the couples interview alone. The next time I need a firm commitment from Rick I'm tempted to staple a note with the date to his shirt so when he comes in contact with someone they can help me remind him.

One evening after dining with friends at a local seafood restaurant my husband, Lloyd, asked me, "Hey, how old am I anyway?"

"You're fifty-five," I told him without hesitation.

"Are you sure?" he said.

"Most definitely," I assured him, thinking he must be kidding.

He shook his head. "Hmm. I thought I was fifty-four."

His expression told me he was serious. So I decided I'd better spell is out for him. "Lloyd," I began. "You were born in 1954. This is 2010. Your birthday is not for five months. Then you'll turn fifty-six."

Lloyd stopped at a traffic light and turned toward me and asked again, "Are you sure?"

"Call your mother," I suggested when I sensed this conversation was going in circles.

HANK AND ELECTRONICS

My husband, Frank, loves to watch movies at home. He'd been waiting for the release of "The Incredible Hulk" and had purchased the Blu Ray version from the local electronics store early in the morning on the day it became available.

When I arrived home from work that afternoon to enjoy it with him, he popped it into the player and was very disappointed the movie would not play. Despite inserting and ejecting it multiple times, it still wouldn't work. He was more than a little irked. He called the electronics store. They told him the DVD was probably okay but he'd need to download an update for the Blu Ray player.

Frank couldn't believe this news. He grumbled that his player was less than three months old. He grabbed his truck keys and headed back to the store with the movie in his hand.

Although I am not very computer literate, I was intrigued by the idea of trying to download a new program onto our player. After Frank left, I followed the on-line instructions which took less than fifteen minutes to install.

By the time Frank got home, the player was "good to go." Unfortunately, while Frank was at the store, he felt compelled to purchase the latest and greatest Blu Ray player "because he needed it."

Frank seemed genuinely disappointed the "old" player was now completely updated but quickly rationalized we needed a player for our bedroom anyway. The cost of the DVD experience was $325.

I am constantly amazed at the level of curiosity of the Hanks in my life. When we moved into our new house, we decided to install an electronic fence around the perimeter of our backyard to train our three Labradors to stay on our property.

I have *never* considered trying out the dog training collars on myself but on three separate occasions I have witnessed a Hank intentionally trying it. None of them actually believed it would create an unpleasant sensation.

The first incident occurred during the construction of the fence. The youngest member of the installation crew decided, with the encouragement from the other guys, to give it a try. I was sweeping the driveway when I heard a shrill scream. I ran to the backyard to discover the young man rubbing his neck and howling as his co-workers hollered with laughter.

Later, after we moved in, my husband, Charlie, couldn't tell if the batteries in the dogs' collars needed to be changed so he decided to snap a collar on his own hand to find out.

Unfortunately, he also reasoned since the intensity for our eighty-pound dogs was set only on the number two setting, and he was so much larger than the Labs, he'd up the setting to a nine. The jolt he received was enough to knock the collar from his hand as he yelped.

I grabbed a mop to knock the device out of the "hot zone" in case my contact with it set it off again. Obviously the batteries still held a charge.

The third collar test happened when my uncle Joe helped plant some trees in our front yard. He'd noticed the dogs stayed obediently on the other side of the fence even though the gate was left open. He wondered just how those collars worked.

I suggested he not experiment with the things. Luckily he's not the member of my family who has a pacemaker. Fortunately all three men recovered quickly. And the dogs? Each of them experienced a single jolt on a mild setting. That was all it took. They learned their lessons and have never ventured from our backyard.

It's easier to train dogs than Hanks.

My husband, Paul, loves electronic gadgets. He simply had to have this headset that plugs into a telephone receiver, allowing him to be "hands free."

I noticed the freedom at times gave Paul a sense he was not tethered to a phone. On one occasion, he grabbed a fly swatter and leaped from his chair to chase the insect.

He succeeded in nearly hanging himself, becoming disconnected from his call, knocking his laptop to the ground, and dumping his coffee from a nearby table.

He missed the fly and cursed as he stumbled to his phone to plug himself back in.

I was glad when Bluetooth became available!

Hank and Housework

These pages were left intentionally blank.

Hanks don't help with housework.

They create housework.

HANK AND HOME PROJECTS

My husband, Bobby, decided right out of the blue we needed to re-stain our wooden backyard fence. This revelation came the week before our daughter's graduation from high school. He wanted our home to look especially nice for the numerous out-of-town relatives who would be visiting us and attending the celebration party.

Being ever resourceful, and realizing he didn't have a paint sprayer, Bobby reasoned sprayers could be used interchangeably. He carefully poured the gallon of stain into the weed-killer tank, strapped it onto his back, attached the weed sprayer to the tank and confidently went out to begin the project.

I stood by, inside at the kitchen window, and noticed Bobby was not mindful we were experiencing very strong winds. The trees in our backyard were more than swaying in the "breeze."

It was only after he'd completed the job, he realized he'd inadvertently also painted the bricks of our home, the sidewalk, and his car.

Clean-up crews were hired as soon as the wind (and laughter) died down. He took his car to the body shop to be repainted, keeping the original color, despite the neighbor's suggestion Bobby go for the "camo" look with the splattered brown paint accents.

My husband, Kyle, prides himself on the fact he was on the job site daily as our new home was being built. After we moved in and had placed our furniture in all the rooms, it became apparent we did not have enough storage space in the garage for all of his childhood treasures.

Kyle decided to store his multiple boxes in our new attic. We had quite a spirited debate about what area of the attic was best to access and safe enough to build shelves. Kyle reasoned there was sub-flooring throughout the entire cavernous area.

He masterfully carried armfuls of boards and an electric saw up the steps to begin his new construction project. While still carrying one of the long boards between the rafters, his weight shifted and he "tested" the sub-flooring.

Much to his dismay, the new "sub-flooring" turned out to be the plaster board of the ceiling above our new king-sized bed.

Luckily for Kyle, as he rapidly exited our attic, the board he held partially and temporarily halted his fall before he bounced on our bed.

Fortunately, the only thing he injured was his pride.

While installing an electronic dog fence around our backyard, it was necessary to connect the wires to the electric supply to our house. I was quickly dispatched to Home Depot to buy a new drill bit over a foot long to drill through the masonry of our home.

My husband, Charlie, picked a spot less than six inches away from the 220 Volt Meter attached to the back of the house rather than plugging it into a nearby outlet as I suggested. He reasoned the dogs would probably unplug the cord even though it was protected by a wooden fence and set of trashcans. Charlie was determined, although he had no previous experience in wiring, he could successfully complete his project.

I stood by for quite a long time, witnessing Charlie's repeated attempts to drill through the house. I held my cell phone in my hand and had already dialed 9 – 1 – so I only would need to punch in one more number in the event he contacted a live wire. He was not amused when I grabbed a broom with a wooden handle to beat him away from the current should that become necessary.

Finally, Charlie had to admit this was one project that got the best of him. He'd broken his new drill, put several holes into our house, and scared me for the better part of an afternoon. He reluctantly called an electrician. The man arrived the following day.

After surveying the situation he pushed the ball cap back further on his head and looked directly at my husband. "You could save yourself a bundle of money," he told him. "There's an outlet just behind those trashcans. Why don't you just plug it in there?"

Why, indeed, I thought? It all seemed so simple coming from a professional.

Charlie readily agreed and took the man's advice.

Our daughter's wedding was rapidly approaching. In just three days, family would start to arrive. Early that morning I had commented to my husband, Eric, my shower water was only slightly warm and I planned to call a plumber.

Eric had recently returned from getting his hair groomed for the wedding and picking up his tux. He felt since our budget was tight there was no need to call a professional. He could take care of what he suspected involved our water heater.

He proceeded to the attic and crawled into position next to the heater. He couldn't tell if the gas pilot light was lit. Not remembering to bring a flashlight, he pulled his small cigar lighter from the pocket of his jeans. Somehow he made an adjustment to the gas valve at the same time his lighter came in contact with the igniter.

From downstairs I heard an ominous "Whoosh!" sound.

Moments later, Eric appeared in the kitchen. I looked up from the lasagna I was preparing to discover most of the facial hair had been scorched from Eric's face. He leaned over the sink, took off his glasses, and rubbed his face. Pieces of singed hair fell into the sink. His skin looked as if he had a bad sunburn. Although his eyebrows were mostly missing, thankfully his glasses prevented injury to his eyes.

He washed his face and without saying another word got back into his car and returned to the barber. When he came home an hour later, he had an all new look. The goatee and mustache he'd had for over ten years were missing and his hair was shorter than I'd ever seen on him.

Our daughter still refers to the incident as "the time Dad whooshed himself right before my wedding." In the pictures most people don't recognize Eric until they notice his boutonniere.

My husband, Adam, enjoys "doing" projects during the weekend. Frequently, he asks his father and brother who live nearby to help him.

His "project days" usually begin in a similar manner. Adam wants to get an "early" start, and he arranges for his helpers to meet at 9:00 at our house. Adam gets up at five till nine and is surprised to discover the other two men already having coffee in our kitchen. He joins the others at the table to create the "list." After careful consideration, he writes at least twenty tasks that need his immediate attention.

The group decides to accomplish the most complicated job first. After much in-depth discussion, it is determined no one has the proper power tools (toys) or supplies. One of the men will then recall he thinks he has one of the tools, but can't remember where he put it or he thinks he might have loaned it to someone.

Next the trio piles into the truck and heads to Home Depot, agreeing to just buy the essentials. Adam assures me they'll be back in less than an hour. I know better.

After walking the aisles at the store, usually multiple times, looking for the same item, they make their purchases and determine they're really hungry. Lunch is next on their agenda. Adam's brother enjoys eating at a Mexican restaurant in a nearby town. Rationalizing on a work day they wouldn't have time to eat there, and since it's only twelve-thirty, they head out-of-town.

They return to the house around three, not able to comprehend what's happened to the time. Adam reasons now there won't be enough daylight left to complete the project they'd initially planned to do. Instead, he suggests they clean out the cabinets in the garage just so the entire day won't be wasted.

When I go out an hour later to offer them some iced tea, all three of the men are sitting in lawn chairs. A stack of thirty-foot tape measures still in the boxes along with various sacks of supplies are piled on the garage floor. The materials look suspiciously like the ones they'd purchased the previous month to complete the same project. The cabinets are empty.

The men are talking about firing up the grill to make steaks for dinner. But, Adam realizes, we don't have meat.

It looks like a trip to the grocery is in order. I call my mother-in-law and sister-in-law who have already prepared various salads. I confirm I have the dessert. I also ask the women if they need a tape measure. We have eight extras.

Another productive Saturday. I'm just glad the weather didn't spoil their plans.

My dad, Louis, recently retired after being an accountant for over forty years. Deciding our large family home was too much to maintain, he and Mom sold the house and bought a nice-sized condo in an all-seniors complex.

Not too long after moving in, Dad wanted to use the long wall in the hallway to hang his large collection of family pictures. Dad has the reputation of being excellent with figures but quite the opposite with handyman efforts.

After going out to purchase a new drill, Dad attempted to put wall anchors up. He only succeeded in breaking his drill bit. Not once. Not twice. But three times. Thinking there must be a stud or something else behind the plaster preventing his drill from penetrating the wall, Dad returned to the store and bought a four-pack of bits. Upon going back home, he called my husband, Tyler, for assistance.

"Show me what you're doing," Tyler instructed.

Mom, Tyler, and I watched as Dad attempted to drill through the wall, only to break another bit.

"See," Dad said in frustration. "That's exactly what keeps happening."

"And now I understand why," Tyler told him. He took the drill from Dad and showed him a small lever on the side. "You've had the drill set on 'reverse'. Instead of penetrating the plaster, the drill bit came the wrong way."

"What's that, you say?" Dad said, clearly intrigued by the complexity of his drill. "You're telling me this thing goes in reverse, like a car? Who in their right mind would want to use a drill like that?"

Tyler put in another bit and handed the drill back to Dad. "People use the reverse position when they want to remove a screw from the wall or a board. It's easier than doing it by hand. Go ahead. Try it in this position."

Dad did as instructed. His first wall anchor successfully implanted in the wall. We all clapped.

"I don't understand why the manufacturer would have these things set to go the wrong way right out of the box," he grumbled. He turned to Tyler. "If you hadn't come along, I was about ready to head back to the store to return the thing."

On the way back to our house, Tyler and I decided a great Christmas gift for Dad would be a book on basic home repairs with instructions on how to operate simple power tools.

Hank and the "Boys"

AKA:
Hanks . . . Working, Playing, Thinking (?) Together

My husband, Barry, and his friends never fail to amaze me with their antics.

Barry recently went on a business trip to Myrtle Beach and returned with a bottle proclaiming the dark red liquid inside was "the second hottest sauce in the world."

The evening he returned from the trip his three good friends came over to our house to watch a hockey game on TV. Naturally, before the game started, Barry pulled out the bottle of sauce.

He proudly passed the bottle around to his friends then encouraged each of them to just "try a little." I was intrigued with this substance which fully commanded the attention of all four men. One whiff convinced me that there was absolutely no way I'd ever touch the stuff.

One by one each of the men however decided to give it a try. Although they watched the reactions of those who'd sampled the sauce before them, no one passed on this epic experience. The first man licked a small amount of the potent stuff from his finger then immediately ran to the refrigerator and drank milk directly from the carton.

After the second taste-tester tried a sample on the edge of a cracker, he dashed to the kitchen sink, turned the water on full blast and stuck the sprayer into his mouth.

Barry's third friend tried only a tiny amount that required him to fan his hand back and forth in front of his outstretched tongue for several minutes.

At last it was Barry's turn. Before he could raise his finger to his lips, I ran over to him and wiped the stuff off with a wet dish towel.

All four men watched the hockey game in silence for the first period. No one touched the chips and queso I'd prepared. They did consume a total of two gallons of iced tea.

Our neighbor, Clay, decided he wanted to install a basketball hoop on the side of his house. Clay has a reputation of being the guy in the neighborhood who has difficulty using the power sprayer on the hose to clean grass from his front walk.

Although the box containing the hoop said some assembly was required and the clerk at the sporting goods store had given him the option of having it preassembled for $20.00, Clay thought he would save the money. He knew he was up to the challenge.

I began walking my dogs around the block in the late afternoon. As I circled the block for the first time, I noticed Clay seemed to have multiple boxes ripped open on his driveway. He was bending over them, seemingly intent on surveying the contents of each box.

Our street is quite long and from the time I spotted Clay in the driveway until long after I had passed his house, he didn't appear to be making any progress. He just kept staring at the boxes.

Since I have four dogs, I thought it would be worthwhile to exercise each one of them individually instead of attempting two at a time. Back at my house I leashed the second dog and started my trek once again. Our block is over one mile long, up and down hills.

When I passed Clay's house for the second time, I noticed multiple neighbors seemed to have gathered in the driveway across the street. Three men sat in lawn chairs. They laughed, whooped, and hollered, seeming to enjoy the "show."

By the time I retrieved my third dog and once again passed Clay's house I stopped to chat with the group of onlookers.

"How are things going with Clay?" I asked.

One man slowly shook his head and referred to some writing he'd scrawled on the back of a Home Depot receipt. "Well, let's see," he said, examining his notes. "So far Clay has downed three diet Cokes, gone into his house four times, and has attempted to put a screw in the backboard on three separate occasions without success."

Another neighbor chimed in, "Yes, but he has been successful in putting the net actually on the hoop which should be the last step of the project."

This comment was met with more howls of laughter. Another man joined the group with his chair and a cooler of drinks. A woman appeared, carrying some chips and pretzels.

"Look! There he goes again," someone shouted. "That makes his fifth trip back into the house."

I observed the man taking notes make another entry. He shook his head again and commented, "You should have seen him when he finally got up the nerve to put up the ladder on the side of his house. He was shaking so badly I thought he was going to fall off and land in his wife's rose bushes."

Intrigued by the circus-like antics, I reluctantly tugged on the leash and resumed my walk. By the time I came around for my fourth and final trip, I noticed Clay's wife was summoning him into the house. It appeared he'd lost track of the time and they were now late for a dinner engagement. I stopped across the street where collectively the onlookers held their breath, obviously waiting to see what Clay would do next.

We all watched Clay walk into the house. Moments later he and his wife and kids left in their mini van. All his tools and the pieces of his project lay scattered on his driveway and lawn.

"It's time to move, boys," the man who'd been taking notes announced.

I watched as the men got up from their chairs and as a group walked across the street. Not able to pull myself away, and now tired from walking nearly four miles, I sat in one of the vacated chairs.

In rapid fashion, the men worked skillfully and had the entire basketball court assembled and mounted on the side of the garage. They gathered Clay's tools and put them away as he had forgotten to lower his garage door upon leaving.

The woman who'd contributed the snacks arrived with a huge red bow. One of the men got up on the ladder and tied the bow to the hoop. I was impressed.

This just goes to show Hanks really do take care of their own kind.

HANK, EVER OBSERVANT

My husband, Russell, had been waiting quite a few months for his new car to arrive. He has been interested in having a convertible for as long as I have known him. He was intrigued when Volkswagen came out with a convertible model with a top that actually came out of the trunk and covered the passenger compartment as a hard shell top. He quickly ordered one and waited for it to arrive.

Two weeks after the big day he decided to go to the office on a Sunday afternoon to do some additional paperwork that simply couldn't wait another day. Not wanting to run the risk of damaging the front end of his new vehicle on the steps by the private entrance to the building, Russell carefully backed into the spot.

He still claims to this day the trouble all started because his office manager, who had also decided to put in extra weekend hours, "stole" his usual parking spot. Although parking spaces are not designated in the private employee lot, Russell would frequently park across three parking slots when he needed to "just run in" for his usual 2 – 3 hours of catch up paperwork.

He also wanted to minimize the amount of work necessary for him to carry his large armful of papers into the office and therefore he had backed up as far as possible into the parking space. At this point he observed some gathering dark clouds and decided it looked like it might rain within the next hour or so. He thought it would be wise to put up the top for his car.

Russell had not reasoned it was necessary for him to have clearance space in order for the hard shelled top to be propelled out of the trunk and over the passenger area. As he pushed the buttons and marveled at the new technology, he was amazed when he started to hear an unfamiliar thud.

When the car top came out of the trunk it not only came in contact with the employee picnic table on the adjacent patio it had flipped it onto its side, causing significant damage. He circled the vehicle several times and determined the back portion of the hood and the activation mechanism for the roof now were obviously in need of repair.

Russell was initially not enthusiastic to think the employees had "moved" the picnic table to such an obviously unsuitable spot. He decided to address his concern the following day.

On Monday morning Russell called a meeting. He was quickly informed that everyone, including the executives of the office, had approved relocating the picnic table from its previous position from the side yard of the building to that particular location over three years ago.

After my sister and niece had visited me from Texas, as a thank you for having them, my sister sent me a flower arrangement with a balloon that said, "I Love You!" It was lovely and I set it on the island in my kitchen where I could see it often. Just to be a little devilish, I removed the card, saying who had sent it.

Eight days after I received it, my husband had still not asked me who had sent the flowers and the loving message. I spoke with my sister that evening and her comment was, "Gee, maybe he thinks he sent them and he's waiting for you to thank him for them."

Could it be? Knowing my husband, it was worth considering the possibility!

Recently I attended a medical conference in which as part of the events there was a golf tournament. This activity was well attended by close to 100 people.

As we arrived the coordinator instructed each of us to find our assigned golf carts which already held our clubs. On the front of each of the 50 carts was a sign indicating which hole we were supposed to begin.

As we sat in our respective carts, the woman who served as our coordinator used a megaphone to give us last minute instructions. Our attention was diverted when a lone golf cart came off the course and headed directly toward our large group. The driver stopped just shy of the first cart. He looked up and down the line of carts, then asked the coordinator, "You getting these people ready to golf?"

As I sat in cart number three, it was all I could do not to respond, "No, we're all here to see if you broke the course scoring record." But then I stopped and considered the source. The man was definitely a Hank.

My husband, Marty, volunteered to help me plant flowers and spread mulch in the landscape beds at my office. I was grateful for the help and the blooms looked wonderful.

Two weeks later, Marty stopped by the office and noticed a few weeds had started to peek through the mulch. I assured him after work I'd go out and pull out the weeds. Marty reasoned it would be far more effective if he sprayed the pesky weeds. I was a little worried, but he persisted he knew what he was doing.

Two weeks after he'd sprayed, the only thing left in my flower beds was the mulch. Initially Marty thought the reason all the plants had died was because they were not getting enough water. I suspected this was not the cause since I'd faithfully watered them every three days.

I tried to replant but absolutely nothing seemed to be able to survive in the mulch. The next season exactly the same thing happened. After planting the lovely flowers, within a few days, they first drooped then shriveled.

Apparently, the weed-killer Marty had used prevents the growth of everything for a long, long time. Marty is no longer allowed to spray anything in the flower beds either at my office or our home. Now the blooms are gorgeous and the weeds . . . they're easy to pull.

HANK THE CRIMINAL

During late October of their senior year in high school, a friend of my son, Brandon, decided "just for fun" he would abscond with over 1,000 election signs. My son agreed to take part in the prank. Neither boy realized their act was a felony.

As they "worked" under the cover of darkness, the boys were approached by one of the candidates who asked them politely not to remove his signs, but encouraged them to remove all of those of his opponent.

This request seemed like unfair play to the boys. Since both boys were over eighteen, they decided this man wouldn't be getting their votes. The man went on to explain how much he had invested in the signs.

The boys hadn't considered someone had actually paid for the yard signs. With the back of Brandon's truck as well as the Jeep of his friend filled to the brim, the boys had second thoughts about their caper.

Not knowing what to do with their stash, they finally decided to deposit all of them in the front yard of their elderly English teacher.

Late one spring, my younger son, Justin, his "best" friend and another boy decided to spend the night at the home of a fourth boy. Per their usual routine, they ordered a pizza. When it was delivered they discovered by pooling all of their money they had just enough to cover the cost of the food but nothing left to even rent a movie.

They sat around for a short while until the "host" friend had a brilliant idea. This involved filling the empty pizza box with dog poop, sneaking over to a neighbor's house, putting it at the front door, ringing the doorbell, and then lighting the box on fire.

The boys had targeted a particular home because it had a large concrete area at the front door and no bushes or trees in the immediate vicinity of the house. Justin later told me it seemed "safer" as the group did not want to cause the house to burn to the ground.

My son and his friends then hid in the bushes of the house across the street in case no one was home they could run over and stamp out the flames. A man was home. He answered the door and jumped up and down several times on the box. Having put out the fire, despite the putrid odor coming from the box, the man took it inside his house.

The boys returned to the "host" house and had just settled in the family room to watch a movie on cable TV when the phone rang. Upon answering, the friend was shocked when a distinctly adult male voice asked, "Is your mother at home?"

The young male replied she was home but asleep and offered to take a message.

He held the phone from his ear so his friends could hear the conversation. The caller continued, "I know you boys just set dog poop on fire on my front porch. If you don't get your mother on the phone right now, I'm going to call the police."

The boys were utterly amazed they'd been caught. As the host boy went to get his mother, the other three discussed whether or not the act would earn them a police record.

After a brief conversation with the mother of the house, the neighbor appeared at the front door. He lectured the boys sternly about the amount of damage they might have caused and reminded them of the long term repercussions if he decided to call the authorities.

The boys apologized profusely and offered to mow the man's grass until the school began in September. After shaking hands with each of the boys and turning to leave, the host boy ventured to ask, "How did you know it was us?"

The man turned to face the group and told them, "It was really easy. I just read your name, address and phone number from the side of the pizza box."

A former male co-worker who was a known trouble-maker was finally fired from his job. He left work in a huff and went home to pick up his wife and son. Following this, he drove six hours to his hometown in Missouri, and of all things, decided to rob a bank.

He'd forgotten he was still wearing his uniform with not only the name of the company but also his own name clearly stitched on the front pocket.

My husband, Josh, and I were watching the news on television early one morning when we saw an interesting story. The newscaster relayed the incident of a young man who had been witnessed wandering around his neighborhood for quite some time in the wee hours of the morning.

According to the news account, the man decided to break into a local business in the middle of our sleepy little town. This man apparently did not have a previous police record. As a novice criminal, he chose to enter the building through the panel in the garage door he "kicked in."

After neatly stacking all of the things he wanted to steal by the back door, he became increasingly nervous with his new "career" path and decided to enter the bathroom. While sitting on the throne, he didn't notice the door had automatically locked behind him. With no windows, there was no escape.

The neighbors had become concerned when they saw increased activity in the lot around this building and had called the police to investigate.

Upon their arrival, the police officers found evidence of illegal entry but were not able to locate anyone in the building. When they noticed the materials neatly stacked by the back door, they decided to investigate further and found the young criminal still with his "drawers down" locked in the bathroom.

Hank in Training

Our son, Matt, decided while my husband and I were out of town recently, as he was the man of the house, a few things needed to be done.

It had been raining for quite some time and our grass was almost going to seed. Matt dutifully gathered our four dogs from the backyard into the laundry room and decided he would take on the task of mowing the grass.

Even though Matt is in his early twenties, it had been a rare occurrence for him to participate in yard care at our house. High school then college sports had taken up most of his spare time, or so he had always claimed.

Matt called us enthusiastically after the project was done to report he really enjoyed mowing the grass and the yard looked much better. I was very impressed and felt confident the decision to vacation in Florida had been an excellent idea for many reasons. Among them, our son was assuming the responsibility of watching everything at home and had risen to the occasion to actually perform yard work.

It was not until we had returned from our trip the whole story became apparent.

My father, who lives in the house directly behind ours, inadvertently mentioned Matt had really seemed to enjoy cutting the grass. So much so he'd done it twice during the five days we'd been away.

Apparently, Matt had set off on our riding lawnmower and had not noticed even though the grass was exceedingly high, the mower was only cutting about an inch of grass. As he was parking the mower back in the garage, his grandfather arrived to ask when he was going to cut the grass.

Thinking the older guy must be going daft, Matt explained he had just finished with the grass.

My father laughed as he recalled the incident. He went on to tell me he'd asked Matt to step off the mower and take a little walk with him. Dad clearly demonstrated the unusually high grass that completely covered the tops of their shoes. When they came back to the garage, Dad showed Matt the lever to lower the mowing deck. Matt had cut the entire half acre with the blade in the highest position, allowing the grass to remain close to its "pre-mowed" height.

That being the case, Matt had the opportunity to drive to the gas station to purchase additional fuel for the lawnmower. He spent the next two hours whirling around the yard with the blade set at the proper height. Now when he walked through the backyard he no longer was in higher than ankle deep grass.

Like quite a few fourteen-year-old boys, my son, Darin, wore braces. Also, like many others, Darin frequently ate foods from his "no no" list provided by the orthodontist. After eating a large amount of caramel corn, it became necessary for us to visit Dr. Adams to repair a bracket.

On the day of our appointment, Darin awoke with a dreaded cold. Although I thought after the office visit it would be in my son's best interest to stay home from school for the remainder of the day, Darin told me that wasn't an option. He had a history test scheduled during his fifth period class. He went on to explain it was this teacher's policy if a student was absent on a test day, instead of receiving the usual multiple-choice type test, students who were absent would take an essay test.

I felt Darin's forehead and determined he wasn't feverish. If he wanted to take a test, I'd deliver him to school. But, first, I decided, I'd stop at a local pharmacy and purchase some over-the-counter medicine to help relieve his cold symptoms.

Darin waited in the car to do some last minute studying, which was curious to me, but I chose not to comment. I dashed through the CVS, picked up a bottle of DayQuil and grabbed a bottle of NyQuil just in case Darin needed nighttime relief from his cold.

I handed Darin the bag with both bottles then headed toward his school while he pulled out the bottle of medicine. I cautioned him to read the label and take just the prescribed amount for his weight. He reminded me he was no longer a child.

Darin sat quietly as I negotiated noon traffic on our twenty mile trip. I assumed he was studying, but when I pulled up to the curb of the school I saw he was sound asleep. It only took me a few seconds to determine Darin had taken the nighttime medicine instead of the non-drowsy variety. He was zonked. When he awoke in time for dinner, he came downstairs with a frown on his face and a history book in his hand.

A friend of mine's ten-year-old son plays on a select basketball team. His coach happens to be the husband of the OB/GYN who delivered the boy.

When his mother informed him his coach's wife was the "baby doctor" who had helped him into the world, the young boy responded, "Cool, I can hardly wait to tell my coach."

When my friend questioned why this information was so "cool" to relay, the child replied, "Because that makes him my step-dad."

My friend was flabbergasted and questioned what in the world would cause him to come to that conclusion.

Her son informed her, "Well, because she delivered me and he is her husband, that would make him like sort of my dad, right?"

As my friend tried to follow this illogical conclusion, she suddenly realized how fortunate she was. She was very thankful her son had shared his theory of "relativity" with her instead of relating it to his buddies or the teachers at his school.

On a recent holiday cruise, our family of four joined another family of four at the airport. The adults found it disconcerting our son, Brandon, who is twenty-four and has completed his graduate program had come to the airport wearing his jeans, tee shirt, and cap but had forgotten an important element of clothing. His belt.

Brandon had recently lost fifteen pounds and was having quite a bit of difficulty keeping his pants up. With both of the fathers harassing him repeatedly, he decided it was in his better interest to accept a belt in loan. I had an extra one in my carry-on bag. Although it fit him perfectly fine, Brandon seemed embarrassed to wear the shiny purple belt.

Later, after we'd reached our ship and prepared to eat in the formal dining room on the cruise ship, Brandon was surprised to find out even though he had packed a pair of black dress shoes, both shoes were for his right foot.

He was even more amazed to discover it was not comfortable to put a right shoe on a left foot. His attempt to walk down the hall and then to descend the stairs in route to our restaurant was more than comical to watch.

Since on this cruise there were two "formal dress" dinners, Brandon had the options of wearing his tennis shoes or the mismatched pair. Wearing a tux and tennies made quite a fashion statement.

While most adults are able to learn from their mistakes, sadly, that isn't the case with Brandon. Three months after the cruise my husband treated Brandon to a father/son golf trip to celebrate successfully completing his Masters degree.

When the traveling duo arrived at the hotel, Brandon unpacked his suitcase only to discover he'd forgotten to bring any underwear. He had to admit this to his dad who took him to a nearby mall.

Although Brandon is not yet married, his evolution into a full-fledged Hank is almost complete.

When my son, Brody, was twelve years old, he and his best friend, Corey, were having a sleepover at our house. It was close to ten o'clock when I glanced out the front window and noticed the boys' bicycles were still on the sidewalk. I asked them to go put their bikes in the garage, and headed upstairs to take a shower.

A half hour later when I went back downstairs the two boys were nowhere to be found. I called their names inside and then went outside. The first thing I noticed was the bikes were no longer out front. A quick check in the garage showed me the bikes weren't in there either. Clearly the boys had taken off for parts unknown.

I called Corey's mother, hoping the boys hadn't decided to ride their small bikes without lights all the way to his house which involved crossing a major intersection. Corey's mom confirmed my worst suspicion. No. The boys weren't there. So, where were they?

My husband, both of Corey's parents, and I each took our own vehicles to hunt for the boys. We communicated via cell phones and each canvassed different areas. After an hour of looking, there was no sign of the boys. We met back at our house where my daughter waited in case the boys came back. We spent the next hour calling every friend we could think of, inquiring if the boys had shown up at any of their homes. We didn't find the boys but did manage to awaken many families.

Finally, just after one in the morning, a police car pulled up to our curb. As I hurried down the front walk, an officer opened the back door to the cruiser and out scrambled Brody and Corey. The first thing out of Brody's mouth was, "Mom! Did you know you can't open the back doors of police cars from the inside?"

The officers escorted the boys inside our house. "I'll bet you've all been looking for these guys," the female officer said.

I could only nod.

"Go ahead and explain where you've been," she prompted.

"We saw this really bright light. We thought it was from up by our school," Corey added.

"So, we got on our bikes to see where it was." Brody stopped talking and looked down at his shoes.

"Officer Thompson and I spotted the boys hiding in some bushes quite aways from here near the Target store," the burly, gray-haired male officer supplied.

"The Target store!" Corey's mom exclaimed, bringing her hand up to her heart. "That's more than five miles from here!"

"I know!" Corey told her. "We rode and rode and rode."

"What on earth prompted you boys to pull this kind of stunt?" my husband asked.

The boys shrugged in unison. "When we saw the search light we thought something big must be going on," Brody said. Then he yawned. So did Corey.

"The light was set up to announce the grand opening of the new Wendy's next door to Target," the female officer told us. "Apparently, the boys had no idea where they were. They couldn't find their way back home and knew they'd be in trouble. They hid in the bushes when they saw our cruiser."

"We thought we were going to be arrested," Brody whispered.

The male officer stood and looked down at the boys. Using his sternest, deepest voice he said, "Other than being in violation of city curfew regulations, you boys have done nothing to merit a trip down to the police station. However, I would advise you both to issue your most sincere apologies to your parents."

They immediately did so.

The officers shook our hands and left. Eventually, so did Corey and his parents.

Sleep was a long time coming that night. As I starred at the dark ceiling, it occurred to me the boys hadn't even launched into their teen years. Heaven only knew what other late-night adventures lie in store for our young Hanks.

How to Submit YOUR Hank Stories

The Hank Syndrome Chronicles Book Two is already in production. We are looking for additional stories to include these topics as well as those previously explored in this edition:

Hank the Grill Master

Hank in the Hospital

Hank Sick in Bed

Hank and Lawn Work

Hank in the Kitchen AKA Hank Discovers Fire

Hank and the In-laws

Hank Plays Golf

Hank Builds a House

Hank Buys a Car

Hank Goes on a Diet/Gets into Shape

Hank Buys a Computer

Hank's Family Reunion

Hank Plants a Garden

Hank on the Fourth of July

Hank in Middle Life

Hank Chooses a Pet

Hank Goes Skiing

Hank at a Garage Sale

Hank Gets Hungry

Hank at Sam's

Hank and Fireworks

Hank Goes Camping
>   AKA: Hank Discovers Fire Ants

Hank Makes Dinner

Hank Helps Out

Hank and the Remote Control

Hank Hooks up a DVD Player

Hank Does Banking

Hank Does Texas

Hank Does Taxes

Visit our website: www.hankstories.com to contribute your Hank Stories. There is also contest information, book store signing details, and release dates. Each month we award a journal to one lucky contributor. We'll look forward to hearing from you and sharing *your* Hank stories!

The following is a submission from Marie in Chicago. It came in just as we were wrapping up our first edition. It's a great example of just what we're hoping to receive for our future books. Thanks for writing to us, Marie. And, keep on laughing! Your Hank does sound remarkably like ours!

When I first heard of the Hank Syndrome Chronicles, I thought, those sisters must know my husband, Glenn. I knew I had several stories to contribute. But which ones should I choose?

I pondered my decision one morning as I heated water for my Earl Gray tea. Glenn was also in the kitchen, making coffee "his way" as I never can seem to get it strong enough for him.

Not using a container of coffee he had previously opened, Glenn grabbed a fresh bag. In his attempt to open it, he used a little too much force. Ground coffee erupted from the bag, spreading a brown cloud that now covered the kitchen floor.

Mumbling beneath his breath, Glenn went ahead and filled his large coffeemaker with water, leaving a trailing puddle on the counter and rug near the sink. I finished making my tea and joined Glenn who was now reading the newspaper at the kitchen table.

"Would you look at this!" he suddenly exclaimed. "They're having a 25th Anniversary Sale at the Frye's Electronics store. From midnight until three there's 25% off everything. I won't want to miss that!"

I leaned forward in my chair and peered at Glenn over the rims of my glasses. "What on earth do you need from Frye's?" I asked.

"Need?" he scoffed. "I can't think of a single thing. I'll just go to look around."

"Right," I returned. "Then I guess you can just leave your MasterCard at home."

Not choosing to reply, Glenn got up and proceeded to wipe up the coffee grounds with a wet paper towel. Brown streaks now swirled over the white tiled floor. Seemingly oblivious to the mess, he tossed the towel into the trash, poured himself a mug of strong coffee and grabbed his car keys.

"I'll see you tonight after work," he told me, placing a kiss on the top of my head.

"Be careful," I said, watching as he opened the door and entered the garage. Seconds later I was not surprised to see him re-enter the kitchen.

"Forgot my wallet," he announced, walking toward the bedroom.

Hank stories definitely abound at our house. I probably have enough to fill an entire book from the thirty-six years I've spent married to Glenn.

www.ingramcontent.com/pod-product-compliance
Lightning Source LLC
Chambersburg PA
CBHW021220090426
42740CB00006B/302